knitted animal nursery

knitted animal nursery

35 gorgeous animal-themed
knits for babies, toddlers,
and the home

fiona goble

CICO BOOKS
LONDON NEW YORK

Published in 2017 by CICO Books
An imprint of Ryland Peters & Small Ltd
20–21 Jockey's Fields, London WC1R 4BW
341 E 116th St, New York, NY 10029

www.rylandpeters.com

10 9 8 7 6 5 4 3 2 1

Text © Fiona Goble 2017
Design, illustration, and photography ©
CICO Books 2017

A CIP catalog record for this book is
available from the Library of Congress and
the British Library.

ISBN: 978 1 78249 433 1

Printed in China

Editor: Kate Haxell
Designer: Alison Fenton
Photographer: Terry Benson
Stylist: Rob Merrett
Illustrator: Stephen Dew

Art director: Sally Powell
Production controller: Mai-Ling Collyer
Publishing manager: Penny Craig
Publisher: Cindy Richards

contents

chapter 1

cute clothes and **bags** 8

chapter 2

heads, hands, and **tiny toes** 46

chapter 3

for the **nursery** 76

introduction

No one can carry off the super-cute animal look quite as well as babies and toddlers. And I don't think it's ever too early in life to stand out from the crowd—just a little bit. That was the thinking behind the range of patterns in this book, which contains lots of straightforward designs for new and intermediate knitters, and some more challenging ideas for seasoned crafters.

The book is aimed at knitters who want to create something less run of the mill, either for their own little ones or to give as gifts. I've divided the book into three sections. So there are chapters full of clothes and accessories for babies and for toddlers. And there's also a section with items to make for the nursery, including toys, pillows, and rugs.

For babies, you can choose from a frog onesie and matching hat, a gorgeous tiger or bumblebee outfit, and lots more besides. Or you may want to whip up my personal favorite item in the book, a pair of fluffy koala bootees.

For toddlers, there's a striking zebra cardigan, all worked in garter stitch. Also, there are super-bulky bear and rabbit hats that knit up quickly and will definitely help keep out the winter chill. Or, if you're pushed for time, I can thoroughly recommend the cat hairband, which I'm sure you'll be able to finish in two or three evenings. If you'd prefer

to create a toy or an item for the nursery, there are ideas for those as well. So choose from a charming bird mobile, a quirky aardvark, a whale pillow, or even a turtle rug for the nursery floor.

If you're new to knitting, or picking up your needles again after a break, there are patterns that require nothing more than the knitting basics. Most of the hats, the mitts, and the swaddling blanket should all be well within your grasp. But if you want to try your hand at something more advanced, baby and toddler-sized items are always a good place to start. I've included all the instructions you need within the book itself, but you will also be able to find my video tutorials on casting on and binding (casting) off and the basic stitches at www.youtube.com/CICOBooks.

If you can't find the exact yarns I've used, don't worry. But please choose a yarn of the same weight and with a similar fiber content. If you're in doubt, ask at your knitting store or check out the website www.yarnsub.com.

I've loved working on this book and I hope you love making your own versions of the designs. If you have any problems, please contact me via my website, fionagoble.com, and I will do my best to help you out.

Fiona Goble

chapter 1

cute clothes
and bags

tiger
outfit

Big cats don't come much more docile than this. These tiger pants and matching hat are knitted in a luxury yarn that's a dream to knit with and baby friendly. Because it's also washable, it's parent friendly, too. Personally, I don't think there's a new parent in the world who wouldn't be thrilled with this show-stopping ensemble.

yarn and materials

Debbie Bliss Baby Cashmerino (55% wool, 33% acrylic, 12% cashmere) light worsted (DK) yarn

    3 x 1¾oz (50g) balls (137yd/125m) in shade 092 Orange (A)
    1 x 1¾oz (50g) ball (137yd/125m) in shade 300 Black (B)

This quantity will be enough for both the trousers and the hat; 2 balls of orange for the trousers and 1 ball for the hat

13in (33cm) length of ½-in (13-mm) wide elastic

A small amount of standard sewing thread

needles and equipment

US 3 (3.25mm) knitting needles

US 2 (2.75mm) knitting needles

Yarn sewing needle

Standard sewing needle

4 x stitch markers or small safety pins

Medium safety pin (for threading elastic)

gauge (tension)

25 sts and 34 rows in stockinette (stocking) stitch to a 4-in (10-cm) square on US 3 (3.25mm) needles. Note that if you are considering substituting the yarn, this yarn is quite a thin light worsted (DK) and knits up well on these size needles.

measurements

To fit an average 3–6 month (9–12 month) old baby.

The trousers are approx. 12(14)in (30(35.5)cm) long.

The hat has a 13(15)in (33(38)cm) circumference.

For more details on sizes and sizing, see page 114.

abbreviations

See page 126.

to make trousers

Front and back

Make 2

Using US 3 (3.25mm) needles, cast on 58(64) sts in A.
Change to US 2 (2.75mm) needles.
Beg with a k row, work 12 rows in st st.
Mark both ends of last row with a stitch marker or small
safety pin.
Change to US 3 (3.25mm) needles.
Beg with a k row, work 16(24) rows in st st.
Join in B from center of ball.
Next row: K22(24) in B, k14(16) in A, k to end using B from
outside of ball.
Next row: P22(24) in B, p14(16) in A, p in B to end.
Beg with a k row, work 6 rows in st st in A.
Next row: K15(17) in B, k28(30) in A, k in B to end.
Next row: P15(17) in B, p28(30) in A, p in B to end.
Beg with a k row, work 6 rows in st st in A.
Rep last 16 rows once more.
Next row: K22(24) in B, k14(16) in A, k in B to end.
Next row: P22(24) in B, p14(16) in A, p in B to end.
Next row. In A, k27(30), bind (cast) off 4 sts, k to end.
Work on second group of 27(30) sts only.
Next row: Purl.
Next row: Bind (cast) off 2 sts, k to end. *(25(28) sts)*
Beg with a p row, work 3 rows in st st in A.
*Beg with a k row, work 2 rows in st st in B.
Beg with a k row, work 6 rows in st st in A.
Rep last 8 rows, 3(4) times more
Beg with a k row, work 2 rows in st st in B.
Beg with a k row, work 2 rows in st st in A.
Change to US 2 (2.75mm) needles.
Beg with a k row, work 12 rows in st st in A.
Bind (cast) off using one of the US 3 (3.25mm) needles.
Rejoin A to rem 27(30) sts on WS of work.
Bind (cast) off 2 sts, p to end. *(25(28) sts)*
Beg with a k row, work 4 rows in st st.
Work as for first leg from * to end.

Tail

Using US 2 (2.75mm) needles, cast on 10 sts in A.
Beg with a k row, work 8 rows in st st.
Beg with a k row, work 2 rows in st st in B.
Beg with a k row, work 6 rows in st st in A.
Rep last 8 rows twice more.
Break B and cont in A.
Row 33: K1, ssk, k4, k2tog, k1. *(8 sts)*
Row 34: P2tog, p4, p2tog. *(6 sts)*
Row 35: K1, ssk, k2tog, k1. *(4 sts)*
Break yarn and thread through rem sts.

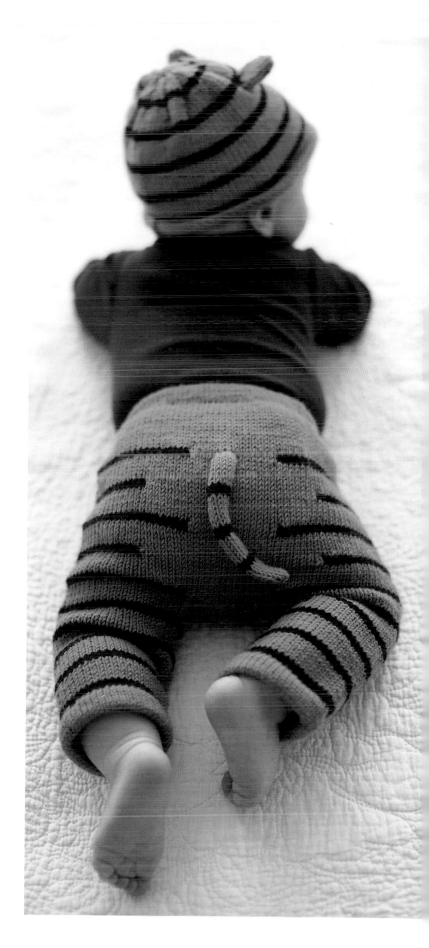

to make hat

Main part

Using US 3 (3.25mm) needles, cast on 84(96) sts in A.

Beg with a k row, work 10(14) rows in st st.

Beg with a k row, work 2 rows in st st in B.

Beg with a k row, work 6 rows in st st in A.

Rep last 8 rows twice more.

Beg with a k row, work 2 rows in st st in B.

Beg with a k row, work 4 rows in st st in A.

Now, working 2 rows st st in A, 2 rows st st in B, then breaking B and working rest of hat in A, AT THE SAME TIME shape crown as folls:

Size 9–12 months only

Next row: [K6, k2tog] to end. *(84 sts)*

Next row: Purl.

Both sizes

Next row: [K5, k2tog] to end. *(72 sts)*

Next and every foll WS row unless otherwise stated: Purl.

Next RS row: [K4, k2tog] to end. *(60 sts)*

Next RS row: [K3, k2tog] to end. *(48 sts)*

Next RS row: [K2, k2tog] to end. *(36 sts)*

Next RS row: [K1, k2tog] to end. *(24 sts)*

Next RS row: [K2tog] to end. *(12 sts)*

Next row: [P2tog] to end. *(6 sts)*

Break yarn and thread through rem sts.

Ear

Make 4

Using US 3 (3.25mm) needles, cast on 8 sts in A.

Beg with a k row, work 6 rows in st st.

Row 7: K1, ssk, k2, k2tog, k1. *(6 sts)*

Row 8: P2tog, p2, p2tog. *(4 sts)*

Bind (cast) off.

to make up hat

Sew back seam of hat using mattress stitch (see page 125).

Place two ear pieces right sides together and oversew (see page 126) round the curved edges. Turn the right way out and slip stitch the cast-on edges together. Make the other ear in the same way. Oversew the ears in position using the photograph as a guide.

Weave in all loose ends.

to make up trousers

Join inner and outer leg seams using mattress stitch (see page 125), keeping markers in position at waist.

Oversew (see page 126) crotch seam.

Turn up just under ¾in (2cm) for the lower hems and oversew in place.

Turn down the waistband so that the cast-on edge meets the row indicated by the markers. Oversew in position, leaving a gap at one side for threading the elastic. Thread the elastic, secure the ends, and sew the gap in the waistband closed.

ladybug
backpack

No self-respecting toddler can do without a backpack these days, to carry around life's little essentials like a favorite toy and a snack for when those hunger pangs strike. And why would you want something plain and boring when you could have a colorful ladybug? The yarn I've used here is available in a great choice of colors. So if classic ladybugs don't tickle your fancy or go with a planned outfit, try different colors to create a customized bug.

yarn and materials

Debbie Bliss Rialto Chunky (100% merino wool) bulky (chunky) yarn
  1 x 1¾oz (50g) ball (66yd/60m) in shade 024 Scarlet (A)
  2 x 1¾oz (50g) balls (66yd/60m) in shade 001 Black (B)

A small amount of off-white light worsted (DK) yarn

3 x ¾-in (20-mm) black buttons

Black sewing thread

needles and equipment

Size US 10½ (6.5mm) knitting needles

Size US 8 (5mm) knitting needles

2 x double-pointed US 8 (5mm) needles

Yarn sewing needle

Large-eyed embroidery needle

Standard sewing needle

gauge (tension)

15 sts and 21 rows in stockinette (stocking) stitch to a 4-in (10-cm) square on US 10½ (6.5mm) needles.

measurements

The backpack is designed for an average 2–3 year old.

The pack itself is 9¾in (25cm) long and the straps are 16½in (42cm) long (unstretched). You could easily make the straps a bit longer or shorter to suit different sizes.

For more details on sizes and sizing, see page 114.

abbreviations

See page 126.

to make backpack

Front

Using US 10½ (6.5mm) needles, cast on 16 sts in A.
*Row 1: Inc, k to last 2 sts, inc, k1. *(18 sts)*
Row 2: Inc pwise, p to last 2 sts, inc pwise, p1. *(20 sts)*
Row 3: K1, m1, k to last st, m1, k1. *(22 sts)*
Row 4: P1, m1 pwise, p to last st, m1 pwise, p1. *(24 sts)*
Rep rows 3–4 twice more. *(32 sts)*
Beg with a k row, work 30 rows in st st.*
Break A and join in B.
Knit 2 rows.
****Beg with a k row, work 4 rows in st st.
Row 45: K1, ssk, k to last 3 sts, k2tog, k1. *(30 sts)*
Row 46: P1, p2tog, p to last 3 sts, p2tog tbl, p1. *(28 sts)*
Rep rows 45–46, 4 times more. *(12 sts)*
Bind (cast) off.

Lower back

Using US 10½ (6.5mm) needles, cast on 16 sts in B.
Work as for front from * to *.
Knit 2 rows.
Bind (cast) off.

Upper back

Using US 10½ (6.5mm) needles, cast on 32 sts in B.
Row 1: Knit.
Row 2: K4, bind (cast) off 2 sts, then k8, bind (cast) off 2 sts, then k8, bind (cast) off 2 sts, k to end. *(26 sts)*
Row 3: K4, cast on 2 sts, [k9, cast on 2 sts] twice, k4. *(32 sts)*
Work as for front from ** to end.

Antenna

Make 2
Using US 8 (5mm) double-pointed needles, cast on
3 sts in B.
Work 8 rows using the i-cord technique (see page 124).
Round 9: Sl1, k2tog, psso. *(1 st)*
Fasten off.

Straps

Make 2
Using standard US 8 (5mm) needles, cast on 65 sts in B.
Knit 2 rows.
Bind (cast) off.

to make up

Sew front and back pieces together using mattress stitch (see page 125) and making sure the upper part of the back overlaps the lower part. Sew on buttons.

Stitch the antennae in place.

Stitch one end of each strap to the corner of the backpack and the other ends just above the center buttonhole on the upper back.

For the eyes, work a coil of chain stitch (see page 124) using off-white light worsted (DK) yarn. For the eye centers and the spots, separate a length of B into two separate strands and use these to embroider a coil of chain stitch.

Weave in all loose ends.

frog
onesie and hat

Who thought that frogs could look this cute? This two-piece outfit is knitted in a skin-friendly and washable yarn that feels smooth and silky soft. We love this vibrant lime green but if you want to go a little wild, you could try one of the more tropical-frog shades, or even use a mixture of colors to customize your own little amphibian.

yarn and materials

Lion Brand Modern Baby (50% acrylic, 50% nylon) light worsted (DK) yarn
- 3 x 2.6oz (75g) balls (172yd/158m) in shade 194 Chartreuse (2 balls for the onesie and 1 ball for the hat)

For the onesie, 1 ³/₈-in (9-mm) baby-friendly snap fastener and sewing thread to match yarn

For the hat, small amounts of black, off-white, and red light worsted (DK) yarns and a small amount of 100% polyester toy filling

needles and equipment

US 7 (4.5mm) knitting needles

US 5 (3.75mm) knitting needles

Stitch holder or spare knitting needle

Yarn sewing needle

Standard sewing needle

Large-eyed embroidery needle

gauge (tension)

22 sts and 32 rows in stockinette (stocking) stitch to a 4-in (10-cm) square on US 7 (4.5mm) needles. Note that if you are considering substituting the yarn, this yarn is quite a thick light worsted (DK) and knits up well on these size needles.

measurements

To fit an average 3–6 month (9–12 month) old baby.

The onesie measures 13¼(15)in (34(38)cm) from the back of the neck to the crotch and is 18(20)in (46(51)cm) around the chest.

The circumference of the hat is 13(14)in (33(35.5)cm).

For more details on sizes and sizing, see page 114.

abbreviations

See page 126.

---

to make onesie

Back

First leg

Using US 7 (4.5mm) needles, cast on 20(24) sts.
Knit 6 rows.
Beg with a k row, work 4(6) rows in st st.*

Next row: K2, m1, k to end. *(21(25)sts)*
Beg with a p row, work 5 rows in st st.
Next row: K2, m1, k to end. *(22(26) sts)*
Beg with a p row, work 3 rows in st st.
Rep last 4 rows once more. *(23(27) sts)*
Next row: K2, m1, k to end. *(24(28) sts)*

Next row: Purl.

Rep last 2 rows twice more. *(26(30) sts)*

Leave sts on stitch holder or spare needle.

Second leg

Work as for first leg to *.

Next row: K to last 2 sts, m1, k2. *(21(25) sts)*

Beg with a p row, work 5 rows in st st.

Next row: K to last 2 sts, m1, k2. *(22(26) sts)*

Beg with a p row, work 3 rows in st st.

Rep last 4 rows once more. *(23(27) sts)*

Next row: K to last 2 sts, m1, k2. *(24(28) sts)*

Next row: Purl.

Rep last 2 rows twice more. *(26(30) sts)*

Body back

Knit across all sts on second leg, inc into first st on first leg and k to end. *(53(61) sts)*

Beg with a p row, work 15(17) rows in st st.

Next row: K2, ssk, k to last 4 sts, k2tog, k2. *(51(59) sts)*

Beg with a p row, work 13(15) rows in st st.

Next row: K2, ssk, k to last 4 sts, k2tog, k2. *(49(57) sts)*

Beg with a p row, work 33(37) rows in st st.

Ridge pattern

Knit 2 rows.

Beg with a k row, work 4 rows in st st.

These 6 rows form the ridge pattern.

Rep ridge pattern once more.

Next row: Bind (cast) off 3 sts, k to end. *(46(54) sts)*

Rep last row once more. *(43(51) sts)*

Next row: Bind (cast) off 2 sts, k to end. *(41(49) sts)*

Next row: Bind (cast) off 2 sts pwise, p to end. *(39(47) sts)*

Rep last 2 rows once more.** *(35(43) sts)*

Rep ridge pattern 4(5) times.

Next row: K12(15), bind (cast) off 11(13) sts, k to end.

Work on 12(15) sts just worked only, leaving rem sts on needle.

Next row: Knit.

Next row: Bind (cast) off 1 st, k to end. *(11(14) sts)*

Next row: Purl.

Next row: Bind (cast) off 1 st, k to end. *(10(13) sts)*

Knit 4 rows.

Bind (cast) off.

Rejoin yarn to rem sts at neck edge of WS of work.

Next row: Bind (cast) off 1 st, k to end. *(11(14) sts)*

Next row: Knit.

Next row: Bind (cast) off 1 st pwise, p to end. *(10(13) sts)*

Beg with a k row, work 4 rows in st st.

Bind (cast) off.

Front

Work as for back to **.

Rep ridge pattern twice (3 times).

Knit 2 rows.

Next row: Knit.

Next row: Purl.

Next row: K14(17), bind (cast) off 7(9) sts, k to end.

Work on 14(17) sts just worked only, leaving rem sts on needle.

Next row: Purl.

Next row: Bind (cast) off 1 st, k to end. *(13(16) sts)*

Next row: Knit.

Next row: Bind (cast) off 1 st, k to end. *(12(15) sts)*

Next row: Purl.

Rep last 2 rows once more. *(11(14) sts)*

Next row: Bind (cast) off 1 st, k to end. *(10(13) sts)*

Next row: Knit.

Beg with a k row, work 6 rows in st st.

Bind (cast) off.

Rejoin yarn to rem sts at neck edge of WS of work.

Bind (cast) off 1 st pwise, p to end. *(13(16) sts)*
Next row: Knit.
Next row: Bind (cast) off 1 st, k to end. *(12(15) sts)*
Next row: Knit.
Next row: Bind (cast) off 1 st pwise, p to end. *(11(14) sts)*
Next row: Knit.
Rep last 2 rows once more. *(10(13) sts)*
Next row: Knit.
Beg with a k row, work 4 rows in st st.
Knit 5 rows.
Bind (cast) off.

Crotch and leg opening
Work on both front and back pieces.
With RS of work facing and using US 5 (3.75mm) needles, pick up and k 48(50) sts along curve of crotch.
Knit 4 rows.
Bind (cast) off.

to make up onesie
Join the right shoulder seam using mattress stitch (see page 125).

Armhole bands
With RS of work facing and using US 5 (3.75mm) needles, pick up and knit 48(54) sts from armpit to armpit along right armhole.
Knit 2 rows.
Bind (cast) off.
Join left side seam using mattress stitch. With RS of work facing and using US 5 (3.75mm) needles, pick up and knit 50(56) sts from shoulder to shoulder.
Knit 2 rows.
Bind (cast) off.

Neckband
For neck opening, with RS of work facing and using US 5 (3.75mm) needles, pick up and knit 48(52) sts.
Knit 2 rows.
Bind (cast) off.

Join right side seam using mattress stitch. Overlap the left front shoulder over the left back shoulder and sew three snap fasteners in place. Overlap the front crotch and leg placket over the back leg placket, and sew three snap fasteners in place on each side.

to make hat

Main part
Using US 7 (4.5mm) needles, cast on 72(78) sts.
Knit 4 rows.
Beg with a k row, work 30(32) rows in st st.
Size 9–12 months only
Next row: [K11, k2tog] to end. *(72 sts)*
Next row: Purl.
Both sizes
Next row: [K4, k2tog] to end. *(60 sts)*
Next and every WS row unless otherwise stated: Purl.
Next RS row: [K3, k2tog] to end. *(48 sts)*
Next RS row: [K2, k2tog] to end. *(36 sts)*
Next RS row: [K1, k2tog] to end. *(24 sts)*
Next RS row: [K2tog] to end. *(12 sts)*
Next row: [P2tog] to end. *(6 sts)*
Break yarn and thread through rem sts.

Eyes
Make 2
Using US 5 (3.75mm) needles, cast on 24 sts.
Row 1: Knit.
Row 2: Purl.
Row 3: [K2tog] to end. *(12 sts)*
Row 4: Purl.
Rep last 2 rows once more. *(6 sts)*
Break yarn and thread through rem sts.

to make up hat
Sew back seam of hat using mattress stitch (see page 125).

Join short edges of eye pieces to form small dome shapes. Stuff lightly and sew in place on the hat, using the photograph as a guide.

Using black yarn, work a coil of chain stitches (see page 124) for the eye centers. Using off-white yarn, work two circles of chain stitch around each eye center. Work the mouth in chain stitch using red yarn.

Weave in all loose ends.

bluebird bib

If you want to jazz up mealtimes—or just want an interesting baby gift that won't take a month of Sundays to complete—this birdy bib is a great choice. It's knitted in a super-soft washable yarn. And while I've made a bluebird, you could easily create something a bit different: a canary would work well, or even a penguin. Check out a bird book for some colorful inspiration.

yarn and materials

Debbie Bliss Baby Cashmerino (55% wool, 33% acrylic, 12% cashmere) light worsted (DK) yarn

　　1 x 1¾oz (50g) ball (137yd/125m) in shade 071 Pool

Very small amounts of black and yellow light worsted (DK) yarns

1 x ½-in (11-mm) snap fastener

needles and equipment

Size US 3 (3.25mm) knitting needles

Yarn sewing needle

Large-eyed embroidery needle

gauge (tension)

25 sts and 34 rows in stockinette (stocking) stitch to a 4-in (10-cm) square on US 3 (3.25mm) needles.

measurements

To fit an average baby up to 12 months old.

The bib is 8in (20cm) long at the front and 7½in (19cm) wide, at the widest point.

abbreviations

See page 126.

to make bib

Main part

Cast on 34 sts.

Row 1: Knit.

Row 2: K3, m1, k to last 3 sts, m1, k3. *(36 sts)*

Row 3: Knit.

Rep rows 2–3 once more. *(38 sts)*

Row 6: K3, m1, k to last 3 sts, m1, k3. *(40 sts)*

Row 7: K3, p to last 3 sts, k3.

Rep rows 6–7, 4 times more. *(48 sts)*

Row 16: Knit.

Row 17: K3, p to last 3 sts, k3.

Rep rows 16–17, 11 times more.

Row 40: K3, k2tog, k to last 5 sts, ssk, k3. *(46 sts)*

Row 41: K3, p to last 3 sts, k3.

Row 42: Knit.

Row 43: K3, p to last 3 sts, k3.

Rep rows 42–43 once more.

Rep rows 40–45 (last 6 rows) twice more. *(42 sts)*

Rep rows 40–41 twice more. *(38 sts)*

Row 62: K12, bind (cast) off 14 sts, k to end.

Work on last group of 12 sts only, leaving other sts on needle.

Next row: K3, p to end.

Next row: K1, k2tog, k4, ssk, k3. *(10 sts)*

Next row: K3, p to end.

Next row: K1, k2tog, k2, ssk, k3. *(8 sts)*

Next row: K3, p to end.

Next row: K1, k2tog, ssk, k3. *(6 sts)*

Next row: K3, p to end.

Next row: K1, k2tog, k3. *(5 sts)*

Next row: K3, p2tog. *(4 sts)*

Next row: K2tog, k2. *(3 sts)*

Next row: K3tog. *(1 st)*

Fasten off.

Rejoin yarn to rem 12 sts on WS of work.

Next row: P to last 3 sts, k3.

Next row: K3, k2tog, k4, ssk, k1. *(10 sts)*

Next row: P to last 3 sts, k3.

Next row: K3, k2tog, k2, ssk, k1. *(8 sts)*

Next row: P to last 3 sts, k3.

Next row: K3, k2tog, ssk, k1. *(6 sts)*

Next row: P to last 3 sts, k3.

Next row: K3, ssk, k1. *(5 sts)*

Next row: P2tog, k3. *(4 sts)*

Next row: K2, ssk. *(2 sts)*

Next row: K3tog tbl. *(1 st)*

Fasten off.

Strap

With RS facing, cast on 16 sts, pick up and knit 10 sts down first side of bib, 14 sts along bound- (cast-) off edge, 10 sts up second side of bib, turn and cast on 16 sts. *(66 sts)*

Knit 5 rows.

Bind (cast) off.

Wing

Make 2

Cast on 6 sts.

Knit 10 rows.

Row 11: K1, k2tog, ssk, k1. *(4 sts)*

Knit 3 rows.

Row 15: K2tog, ssk. *(2 sts)*

Row 16: K2tog. *(1 st)*

Fasten off.

to make up

Oversew (see page 126) the wings in place across the top, using the photograph as a guide.

Using black yarn, work two coils of chain stitch (see page 124) for the eyes. Using a separated strand of black yarn, work straight stitches (see page 124) for the eyelashes. Using yellow yarn, work a "V" shape in chain stitch for the beak.

Using a separated strand of the main yarn, sew the protruding part of the snap fastener on the underside of one side of the neck strap and the corresponding part on the top of the second side of the neck strap.

Weave in all loose ends.

panda
shorts and hat

Babies always look cute dressed in soft pastel shades, but sometimes you just need a change. With their striking monochrome coat, bamboo-munching pandas are one of the world's best-loved mammals, and thanks to this pattern you can transform the little one in your life into an adorable panda cub. The baby-friendly luxury yarn comes in lots of colors so, if the fancy takes you, you could always use the pattern to create a brown bear cub instead, or how about an all-white little polar bear?

yarn

Sublime Extra Fine Merino DK (100% wool) light worsted (DK) yarn

    1 x 1¾oz (50g) ball (98yd/90m) in shade 001 Black (A)

    2 x 1¾oz (50g) balls (98yd/90m) in shade 003 Alabaster (B)

needles and equipment

US 5 (3.75mm) knitting needles

US 6 (4mm) knitting needles

Yarn sewing needle

Pompom maker to make 2½in (6.5cm) pompom, or two cardboard circles each measuring 2½in (6.5cm) in diameter with a 1¼in (3cm) diameter hole in the center.

gauge (tension)

22 sts and 28 rows in stockinette (stocking) stitch to a 4-in (10-cm) square on US 6 (4mm) needles.

24 sts and 30 rows in stockinette (stocking) stitch to a 4-in (10-cm) square on US 5 (3.75mm) needles.

measurements

The shorts and hat set will fit an average 0–3 month (3–6 month) old baby.

The waist of the shorts is 17½(19)in (44.5(48)cm).

The circumference of the hat is 12½(14)in (32(35.5)cm).

For more details on sizes and sizing, see page 114.

abbreviations

See page 126.

to make shorts

Front and back

Make 2

Using US 5 (3.75mm) needles, cast on 50(54) sts in A.

Row 1: [K2, p2] to last 2 sts, k2.

Row 2: [P2, k2] to last 2 sts, p2.

Rep rows 1–2, 3 times more.

Rep row 1 once more.

Break A, join in B, and switch to US 6 (4mm) needles.

Beg with a k row, work 20(24) rows in st st.

Next row: K24(26), m1, k2, m1, k to end. *(52(56) sts)*

Next and every WS row unless otherwise stated: Purl.

Next RS row: K24(26), m1, k4, m1, k to end. *(54(58) sts)*

Next RS row: K24(26), m1, k6, m1, k to end. *(56(60) sts)*

Next RS row: K24(26), m1, k8, m1, k to end. *(58(62) sts)*

Next RS row: Knit.

Next row: P24(26), bind (cast) off 10 sts pwise, p to end.

Work on 24(26) sts just worked, leaving rem sts on needle, and change to US 5 (3.75mm) needles.

*Next row: Knit.

Next row: Purl.

Knit 3 rows.

Next row: Purl.

Next row: K1, [yo, k2tog] to last st, k1.

Next row: Purl.

Bind (cast) off.

With RS facing, rejoin yarn to rem sts.

Rep from * to end.

to make up shorts

Sew the side seams and crotch seam using mattress stitch (see page 125).

Turn up the lower edges of the legs to form a picot edge and slip stitch in place.

To make the tail, use the pompom maker or cardboard circles to make a pompom in A. Trim the pompom and use the tails of yarn to sew it to the back of the shorts.

to make hat

For 0–3 months, work hat on US 5 (3.75mm) needles.

For 3–6 months, work hat on US 6 (4mm) needles.

Cast on 78 sts in A.

Row 1: [K2, p2] to last 2 sts, k2.

Row 2: [P2, k2] to last 2 sts, p2.

Rep last 2 rows twice more.

Break A and join in B.

Beg with a k row, work 18 rows in st st.

Row 25: [K6, k2tog] 9 times, k to end. *(69 sts)*

Row 26 and every WS row unless otherwise stated: Purl.

Row 27: [K5, k2tog] 9 times, k to end. *(60 sts)*

Row 29: [K4, k2tog] 9 times, k to end. *(51 sts)*

Row 31: [K3, k2tog] 10 times, k to end. *(41 sts)*

Row 33: [K2, k2tog] 10 times, k to end. *(31 sts)*

Row 35: [K1, k2tog] 10 times, k to end. *(21 sts)*

Row 37: [K2tog] to last st, k1. *(11 sts)*

Break yarn and thread through rem sts.

Ear

Make 4

Using US 6 (4mm) needles, cast on 7 sts in A.

Beg with a k row, work 4 rows in st st.

Row 5: Ssk, k3, k2tog. *(5 sts)*

Row 6: P2tog, p1, p2tog. *(3 sts)*

Bind (cast) off.

to make up hat

Sew the back seam using flat stitch (see page 126).

For the ears, place two pieces together so that the right sides are on the inside. Oversew (see page 126) the curved edge, leaving the lower edge open. Turn the right way out. Oversew the ears in place using the photograph as a guide.

For the eyes, work two coils of chain stitch (see page 124) using A, leaving a small amount of white showing in the center. For the nose, work a small coil of chain stitch in A.

Weave in all loose ends.

fox sweater

There's a passion for all things woodland these days and I didn't want to be left out. That's why I created this fox motif top, knitted in a luxury cashmere mix yarn that is kind to babies' skin, and is also washable. Wrap-style tops are easy get over a small baby's head, so this is a very practical sweater, as well as being very cute. There are some intermediate knitting skills involved in this project, so you may want to read through the pattern before you start to make sure you are confident with the techniques needed.

yarn

Debbie Bliss Baby Cashmerino (55% wool, 33% acrylic, 12% cashmere) light worsted (DK) yarn

  2 x 1¾oz (50g) balls (137yd/125m) in shade 002 Apple (A)
  1 x 1¾oz (50g) ball (137yd/125m) in shade 067 Sienna (B)
  1 x 1¾oz (50g) ball (137yd/125m) in shade 101 Ecru (C)

A small amount of black light worsted (DK) yarn (D)

needles and equipment

US 5 (3.75mm) knitting needles

Yarn sewing needle

Large-eyed embroidery needle

gauge (tension)

22 sts and 28 rows in stockinette (stocking) stitch to a 4-in (10 cm) square on US 5 (3.75mm) needles. Note that if you are considering substituting the yarn, this yarn is quite a thin light worsted (DK) and knits up well on these size needles.

measurements

To fit an average 3–6 month (9–12 month) old baby. The sweater measures 19(21)in (48(53.5)cm) around the chest.

For more details on sizes and sizing, see page 114.

abbreviations

See page 126.

to make sweater

Right front

Cast on 52(58) sts in A.

Knit 4 rows.

Beg with a k row, work 20(24) rows in st st.

Next row: K2, k2tog, k to end. (51(57) sts)

Next row: P to last 4 sts, p2tog, p2. (50(56) sts)

Rep last 2 rows 6 times more. (38(44) sts)

Next row: K2, k2tog, k to end. (37(43) sts)

Next row: Bind (cast) off 3 sts pwise, p to last 4 sts, p2tog, p2. (33(39) sts)

Next row: K2, k2tog, k to last 4 sts, ssk, k2. (31(37) sts)

Next row: P2, p2tog tbl, p to last 4 sts, p2tog, p2. (29(35) sts)

Next row: K2, k2tog, k to last 4 sts, ssk, k2. (27(33) sts)

Next row: P to last 4 sts, p2tog, p2. (26(32) sts)

Rep last 2 rows 3 times more. (17(23) sts)

Next row: K2, k2tog, k to end. (16(22) sts)

Next row: Purl.

Rep last 2 rows 6(9) times more. (10(13) sts)

Beg with a k row, work 4(4) rows in st st.

Bind (cast) off.

Left front

Cast on 52(58) sts in A.

Knit 4 rows.

Beg with a k row, work 6(10) rows in st st.

Next row: K17(20), work first row of chart, joining in colors as needed, k18(21).

This row sets position of chart.

Cont in st st and work next 13 rows from chart, without shaping.

Cont working final rows of motif from chart then cont in A only, while also beg shaping as folls:

Next row: K to last 4 sts, ssk, k2. *(51(57) sts)*

Next row: P2, p2tog tbl, p to end. *(50(56) sts)*

Rep last 2 rows 6 times more. *(38(44) sts)*

Next row: Bind (cast) off 3 sts, k to last 4 sts, ssk, k2. *(34(40) sts)*

Next row: P2, p2tog tbl, p to end. *(33(39) sts)*

Next row: K2, k2tog, k to last 4 sts, ssk, k2. *(31(37) sts)*

Next row: P2, p2tog tbl, p to last 4 sts, p2tog, p2. *(29(35) sts)*

Next row: K2, k2tog, k to last 4 sts, ssk, k2. *(27(33) sts)*

Next row: P2, p2tog tbl, p to end. *(26(32) sts)*

Rep last 2 rows 3 times more. *(17(23) sts)*

Next row: K to last 4 sts, ssk, k2. *(16(22) sts)*

Next row: Purl.

Rep last 2 rows 6(9) times more. *(10(13) sts)*

Beg with a k row, work 4(4) rows in st st.

Bind (cast) off.

Back

Cast on 54(60) sts in A.

Knit 4 rows.

Beg with a k row, work 34(38) rows in st st.

Next row: Bind (cast) off 3 sts, k to end. *(51(57) sts)*

Next row: Bind (cast) off 3 sts, p to end. *(48(54) sts)*

Next row: K2, k2tog, k to last 4 sts, ssk, k2. *(46(52) sts)*

Next row: P2, p2tog tbl, p to last 4 sts, p2tog, p2. *(44(50) sts)*

Next row: K2, k2tog, k to last 4 sts, ssk, k2. *(42(48) sts)*

Next row: Purl.

Rep last 2 rows 3 times more. *(36(42) sts)*

Beg with a k row, work 18(24) rows in st st.

Next row: Bind (cast) off 10(13) sts, k to end. *(26(29) sts)*

Next row: Bind (cast) off 10(13) sts pwise, p to end. *(16(16) sts)*

Bind (cast) off rem sts.

Sleeves

Make 2

Cast on 39(45) sts in A.

Row 1: Knit.

Beg with a k row, work 10(14) rows in st st.

Next row: K2, k2tog, k to last 4 sts, ssk, k2. *(37(43) sts)*

Size 9–12 months only

Next row: Purl.

Size 3–6 months only

Next row: P2, p2tog tbl, p to last 4 sts, p2tog, p2. *(35 sts)*

Both sizes

Next row: K2, k2tog, k to last 4 sts, ssk, k2. *(33(41) sts)*

Next row: Purl.

Rep last 2 rows 9(12) times more. *(15(17) sts)*

Next row: K2, k2tog, k to last 4 sts, ssk, k2. *(13(15) sts)*

Next row: P2, p2tog tbl, p to last 4 sts, p2tog, p2. *(11(13) sts)*

Next row: K2, k2tog, k to last 4 sts, ssk, k2. *(9(11) sts)*

Bind (cast) off.

to make up

Using mattress stitch (see page 125), join the top parts of the sweater together from the armpits to the neck edges, so that the two sleeves fit between the front and back pieces. Sew the side and sleeve seams using mattress stitch.

Border

With the RS of the sweater facing you, pick up and knit 17 sts up the vertical edge of the right front, 46 sts up the sloping right front edge, 18 sts across the back neck edge, 46 sts down the sloping edge of the left front, and 17 sts down the left vertical edge. *(144 sts)*

Bind (cast) off.

Slip stitch right front to back along side seam. Overlap left over right front and slip stitch in place along side seam.

Using a separated strand of D, work two flattened "V" shapes for the eyes, using the photograph as a guide.

Weave in all loose ends.

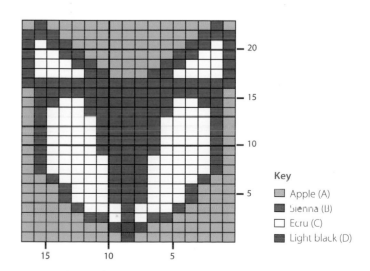

Key

- ▨ Apple (A)
- ▧ Sienna (B)
- ☐ Ecru (C)
- ▦ Light black (D)

kitten bag

Whatever your age, you need an eye-catching bag to tote around life's essentials. This dinky feline bag is double layered so it's really sturdy. I've chosen a lavender bag with a soft taupe lining, but the yarn I've used comes in lots of fabulous shades. Go realistic or choose a color to match a favorite outfit. I've finished this bag off with a knitted flower—but choose a ready-made bow if you prefer, or leave your kitty plain.

yarn and materials

Cascade Pacific Chunky (60% acrylic, 40% wool) bulky (chunky) yarn
  1 x 3½oz (100g) ball (120yd/110m) in shade 26 Lavender (A)
  1 x 3½oz(100g) ball (120yd/110m) in shade 15 Taupe (B)

A small amount of cream light worsted (DK) yarn (C)

Very small amounts of black, dark gray, and light beige light worsted (DK) yarn

2 x ½-in (12-mm) black buttons

1 x medium-size yellow button

needles and equipment

US 10 (6mm) knitting needles

US 9 (5.5mm) knitting needles

US 6 (4mm) knitting needles

Yarn sewing needle

Large-eyed embroidery needle

gauge (tension)

12 sts and 14 rows in stockinette (stocking) stitch to a 4-in (10-cm) square on US 10 (6mm) needles.

measurements

The bag measures 9½in (24cm) across and is 7in (18cm) deep.

abbreviations

See page 126.

to make bag

Bag outer
Make 2
Using US 10 (6mm) needles, cast on 20 sts in A.
Row 1: Inc, k to last 2 sts, inc, k1. *(22 sts)*
Row 2: Purl.
Row 3: K2, m1, k to last 2 sts, m1, k2. *(24 sts)*
Row 4: Purl.
Rep rows 3–4, 4 times more.* *(32 sts)*
Beg with a k row, work 14 rows in st st.
**Row 27: K10, bind (cast) off 12 sts, k to end.

Turn and work on 10 sts just worked only, leaving rem sts on needle.

Next row: P to last 2 sts, p2tog. *(9 sts)*

Next row: Ssk, k to end. *(8 sts)*

Rep last 2 rows twice more. *(4 sts)*

Next row: [P2tog] twice. *(2 sts)*

Next row: Ssk. *(1 st)*

Fasten off.

Rejoin yarn to rem 10 sts on WS of work.

Next row: P2tog, p to end. *(9 sts)*

Next row: K to last 2 sts, k2tog. *(8 sts)*

Rep last 2 rows twice more. *(4 sts)*

Next row: [P2tog] twice. *(2 sts)*

Next row: K2tog. *(1 st)*

Fasten off.

Bag lining

Make 2

Using US 9 (5.5mm) needles, cast on 20 sts in B.

Work as for bag outer to *.

Beg with a k row, work 6 rows in st st.

Break B and join in A.

Beg with a k row, work 6 rows in st st.

Work as for bag outer from ** to end.

Handle

Make 2

Using US 10 (6mm) needles, cast on 5 sts in B.

Beg with a k row, work 24 rows in st st.

Bind (cast) off.

Flower

Using US 6 (4mm) needles, cast on 10 sts in C.

Row 1: [Inc] twice, turn and work on 4 sts just knitted only.

Beg with a p row, work 11 rows in st st.

Next row: K2tog, ssk, lift RH st over LH st. *(1 st)*

***Next row:** K1 into next cast-on st, inc, turn and work on 4 sts just worked only.

Beg with a p row, work 11 rows in st st.

Next row: K2tog, ssk, lift RH st over LH st. ** *(1 st)*

Rep from * to ** 3 more times.

K into first cast-on st to complete final petal. *(2 sts)*

Bind (cast) off 1 st and fasten off.

to make up

Join the side seams of the two main pieces and the two lining pieces using mattress stitch (see page 125). Join the base seams, again using mattress stitch, leaving a gap in the base of the lining, big enough for your hand.

Sew on the buttons for the eyes using black yarn, and using a separated strand of the yarn work some straight stitches (see page 124) for the eyelashes. Using light beige yarn, work a coil of chain stitch (see page 124) for the nose and a line of chain stitch below it. Using dark gray yarn, work some straight stitches for the whiskers.

Insert the lining into the main bag so that the pieces are right sides together. Backstitch the main piece and lining together along the entire top edge. Turn the bag the right way out through the gap in the base of the lining. Close the hole in the lining base. Tuck the lining into the main bag. Slip stitch around the top edge of the bag to ensure a crisp edge.

Join the long sides of the handle pieces together using mattress stitch. Secure the handles in place at the top of the bag, using the photograph as a guide.

Sew the flower in place and add the yellow button center.

Weave in all loose ends.

cow print bib

There's no point in facing the world in some boring old bib when you can sport a unique animal print look instead. That's the thinking behind this cow-print creation, which also happens to be a great way to dip your toe into the world of intarsia color knitting. Of course, you could also knit the bib in a single color if you like, or use it as a template to create a range of other animal looks.

yarn and materials

Sublime Extra Fine Merino DK (100% wool) light worsted (DK) yarn
  1 x 1¾oz (50g) ball (127yd/116m) in shade 003 Alabaster (A)
  1 x 1¾oz (50g) ball (127yd/116m) in shade 013 Jet Black (B)

1 x ½-in (11-mm) snap fastener

Standard white sewing thread

needles and equipment

US 6 (4mm) knitting needles

US G/6 or H/8 (4.5mm) crochet hook (or one of a similar size)

Yarn sewing needle

Standard sewing needle

gauge (tension)

22 sts and 28 rows in stockinette (stocking) stitch to a 4-in (10-cm) square on US 6 (4mm) needles.

measurements

To fit a baby up to 12 months old.

Bib measures 7½in (19cm) wide at top edge and 6½in (16.5cm) deep at the front.

abbreviations

See page 126.

to make bib

Start at bottom edge

Cast on 28 sts using A.
Row 1: Inc, k to last 2 sts, inc, k1. *(30 sts)*
Row 2: Purl.
Row 3: K2, m1, k to last 2 sts, m1, k2. *(32 sts)*
Row 4: Purl.

Row 5: K2, m1, k to last 2 sts, m1, k2. *(34 sts)*
Row 6: Join in B and work row 6 from first row of chart on page 32.
This row sets position of chart.
Follow chart to row 48, increasing 1 st on each RS row up to and including row 15, and using a separate length of B for each black patch. *(44 sts)*

Break all B and cont in A.

Beg with a k row, work 4 rows in st st.

Next row: K15, ssk, turn. *(16 sts)*

Work on 16 sts just worked only, leaving rem sts on needle.

Next row: P2tog, p to end. *(15 sts)*

Next row: K13, ssk. *(14 sts)*

Next row: P2tog, p to end. *(13 sts)*

Next row: K11, ssk. *(12 sts)*

Next and every WS row: Purl.

Next RS row: K10, ssk. *(11 sts)*

Next RS row: K9, ssk. *(10 sts)*

Next RS row: K8, ssk. *(9 sts)*

Next RS row: K7, ssk. *(8 sts)*

Next row: Purl.

Beg with a k row, work 10 rows in st st.

Next row: K2, k2tog, k2, m1, k2.

Beg with a p row, work 3 rows in st st.

Rep last 4 rows once more.

Beg with a k row, work 6 rows in st st.

Next row: K1, k2tog, k2, ssk, k1. *(6 sts)*

Next row: P2tog, p2, p2tog. *(4 sts)*

Bind (cast) off.

Rejoin yarn to RS of work.

Bind (cast) off 11 sts, k to end. *(16 sts)*

Next row: P to last 2 sts, p2tog. *(15 sts)*

Next row: K2tog, k to end. *(14 sts)*

Next row: P to last 2 sts, p2tog. *(13 sts)*

Next row: K2tog, k to end. *(12 sts)*

Next row: Purl.

Rep last 2 rows, 4 times more. *(8 sts)*

Beg with a k row, work 10 rows in st st.

Next row: K2, m1, k2, ssk, k2.

Beg with a p row, work 3 rows in st st.

Rep last 4 rows once more.

Beg with a k row, work 6 rows in st st.

Next row: K1, k2tog, k2, ssk, k1. *(6 sts)*

Next row: P2tog, p2, p2tog. *(4 sts)*

Bind (cast) off.

to make up

Using crochet hook and B double, work an even crochet edging (see page 122) around entire bib.

Sew one part of the snap fastener on the right side of one neck strap. Sew the other part of the snap fastener to the wrong side of the second neck strap so that the strap will fasten around the baby's neck.

Weave in all loose ends.

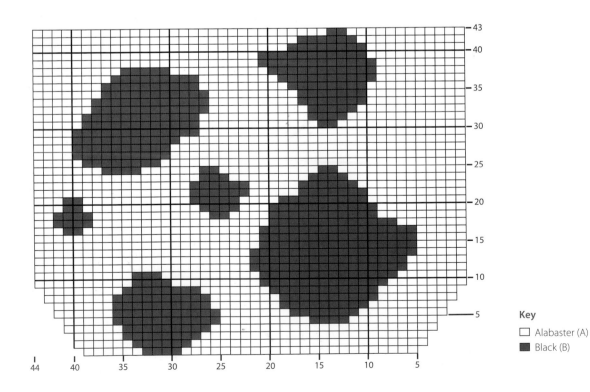

Key

☐ Alabaster (A)

■ Black (B)

zebra striped cardigan

Zebras are one of the most striking creatures in the world—and the little person in your life will look equally striking in this chunky cardigan. It's knitted from the top down, which is one of the easiest ways to knit a cardigan and means you will only have to join the sleeve seams. If you're new to knitting garments, this is a great first or second project.

yarn and materials

Lion Brand Wool Ease (80% acrylic, 20% wool) worsted (Aran) yarn

1 x 3oz (85g) ball (196yd/180m) in shade 153 Black (A)

1 x 3oz (85g) ball (196yd/180m) in shade 099 Fisherman (B)

3 x ¾-in (18-mm) gray buttons

needles and equipment

US 9 (5.5mm) knitting needles
4 x stitch markers or small safety pins
2 x stitch holders
Yarn sewing needle
Large-eyed embroidery needle

gauge (tension)

16 sts and 28 rows in garter stitch to a 4-in (10-cm) square on US 9 (5.5mm) needles.

measurements

To fit an average 12–18 month (2–3 year) old toddler.

The sweater is 24(25)in (61(63.5)cm) around the chest and the length from shoulder to wrist is 9(10)in (23(25.5)cm).

For more details on sizes and sizing, see page 114.

abbreviations

See page 126.

---

to make cardigan

Start at neck

Cast on 51 sts in A.

Knit 4 rows.

Join in B.

Next row: K9, m1 (place marker in st just made), k9, m1 (place marker in st just made), k15, m1 (place marker in st just made), k9, m1 (place marker in st just made), k9. (55 sts)

Next row: Knit.

Next row: [K to marked st, yo, k1, yo] 4 times, k to end. (63 sts)

Next row: Knit.

Rep last 2 rows 11 times more, keeping to the color patt of 4 rows in A, 4 rows in B throughout. (151 sts)

Knit 2 rows.

Next row: [K to marked st, yo, k1, yo] 4 times, k to end. (159 sts)

Next row: Knit.

Rep last 4 rows once (twice) more. (167(175) sts)

Break both yarns.

Divide sts for fronts, back, and sleeves by placing the sts for the two sides of the fronts and for the back on a long length of yarn (either A or B) and the sts for the sleeves on the stitch holders in the following way:

Thread length of yarn through the first 23(24) sts on the needle (first front). Place the next 37(39) sts on a stitch holder (first sleeve). Place the next 47(49) sts on the length of yarn (back). Place the next 37(39) sts on the second stitch holder (second sleeve). Place the rem 23(24) sts on the length of yarn (second front).

Cardigan band (for girl)

With RS facing and A, pick up and k 31(36) sts up the edge of the right front, from the lower edge to the neck edge.
Knit 2 rows.
Row 3: K2, [k2tog, yo, k4] 3 times, k to end.
Knit 2 rows.
Bind (cast) off.
With RS facing and A, pick up and k 31(36) sts down the edge of the left front, from the neck edge to the lower edge.
Knit 5 rows.
Bind (cast) off.

Cardigan band (for boy)

With RS facing and A, pick up and k 31(36) sts down the edge of the left front from the neck edge to the lower edge.
Knit 2 rows.
Row 3: K15(20), [yo, k2tog, k4] twice, yo, k2tog, k2.
Knit 2 rows.
Bind (cast) off.
With RS facing and A, pick up and k 31(36) sts up the edge of the right front, from the lower edge to the neck edge.
Knit 5 rows.
Bind (cast) off.

to make up

Sew sleeve seams using the flat stitch technique (see page 126). Sew on buttons using a separated thread of B.

Weave in all loose ends.

Sleeves

Place the stitches for the first sleeve back on one of the needles, ready to knit on the RS of work and keep to the stripe patt throughout.
Knit 6(8) rows.
Next row: K2, k2tog, k to last 4 sts, ssk, k2. *(35(37) sts)*
K7(9) rows.
Next row: K2, k2tog, k to last 4 sts, ssk, k2. *(33(35) sts)*
Knit 7 rows, ending after 4 rows worked in A.
Knit 2 rows in A.
Bind (cast) off.
Work second sleeve in the same way.

Body

Put all the sts for the two fronts and back on one of the needles. *(93(97) sts)*
Keeping to the stripe patt, knit 22(26) rows, ending after 4 rows worked in A.
Knit 2 rows in A.
Bind (cast) off.

bumblebee outfit

Yellow and black is one of the smartest combinations in nature—and now you can knit something just as stylish for the baby in your life. The outfit is knitted in a gorgeously soft luxury yarn with a touch of cashmere. The shorts have an elasticated waist with a decorative tie. I think this is one of those outfits that will get people talking.

yarn and materials

Debbie Bliss Baby Cashmerino (55% wool, 33% acrylic, 12% cashmere) light worsted (DK) yarn

   2 x 1¾oz (50g) balls (137yd/125m) in shade 300 Black (A)

   1 x 1¾oz (50g) ball (137yd/125m) in shade 083 Butter (B)

This quantity will be enough for both the trousers and the hat. (If you are making the shorts only, you will need 1 ball of black for the smaller size. For the larger size, you may need 2 balls.)

13(14)in (33(35.5)cm) length of ⅝-in (13-mm) wide elastic

A small amount of standard sewing thread

needles and equipment

Size US 2 (3mm) knitting needles

Size US 3 (3.25mm) knitting needles

2 x size US 5 (3.75mm) double-pointed needles

US D-3 (3.25mm) crochet hook (or one of a similar size)

Yarn sewing needle

Standard sewing needle

Medium safety pin (for threading elastic and waist tie)

gauge (tension)

25 sts and 34 rows in stockinette (stocking) stitch to a 4-in (10-cm) square on US 3 (3.25mm) needles. Note that if you are considering substituting the yarn, this yarn is quite a thin light worsted (DK) and knits up well on these size needles.

measurements

To fit an average 3–6 month(9–12 month) old baby.

The shorts are approx. 9¼in (23cm) long.

The hat has a 13½(15½)in (34(39)cm) circumference (measured above ribbed edge).

For more details on sizes and sizing, see page 114.

abbreviations

See page 126.

to make shorts

Front

Using US 2 (3mm) needles, cast on 60(68) sts in A

Beg with a k row, work 8 rows in st st.

Row 9: K25(29), bind (cast) off 2 sts, then k5, bind (cast) off 2 sts, k to end. *(56(64) sts)*

Row 10: P25(29), turn and cast on 2 sts, turn back, p6, turn and cast on 2 sts, turn back, p to end. *(60(68) sts)*

Beg with a k row, work 2 rows in st st.

*Change to US 3 (3.25mm) needles and join in B.

Beg with a k row, work 2 rows in st st

Leave B at side and using A, beg with a k row, work 2 rows in st st.

Rep last 4 rows 11 times more.

Beg with a k row, work 2 rows in st st in B.

Next row: Knit in A.

Next row: Using A, p28(32), cast off 4 sts, p to end.

Work on second group of 28(32) sts only, leaving rem sts on needle.

**Beg with B and keeping to stripe patt set, beg with a k row, work 10 rows in st st

Break B, change to US 2 (3mm) needles and work rem of leg in A.

Next row: Knit.

Next row: [K2, p2] to end.

Rep last row 10 times more.

Bind (cast) off, keeping to the k2, p2 patt.

Rejoin yarn to rem 28(32) sts on RS of work.

Rep from ** to end.

Back

Using US 2 (3mm) needles, cast on 60(68) sts in A.

Beg with a k row, work 12 rows in st st.

Cont as for front from * to end.

Waist tie

Using crochet hook and B doubled, make a 16-in (40-cm) crochet chain (see page 122).

to make up shorts

Join inner and outer leg seams using mattress stitch (see page 125). Oversew (see page 126) crotch seam.

Turn down the waistband so the cast-on edge meets the top of the first yellow stripe on the inside of the shorts. Oversew in position, leaving a gap at one side for threading the elastic. Thread the elastic, secure the ends, and sew the gap in the waistband closed. Thread the cord in and out of the two holes at the front, tie in a bow, and secure the bow with a few stitches.

Weave in all loose ends.

to make hat

Main part

Using US 3 (3.25mm) needles, cast on 84(96) sts in A.

Row 1: [K2, p2] to end.

Rep row 1, 7 times more.

Beg with a k row, work 30 rows in st st.

Size 9–12 months only

Next row: [K6, k2tog] to end. *(84 sts)*

Next row: Purl.

Both sizes

Next row: [K5, k2tog] to end. *(72 sts)*

Next and every foll WS row unless otherwise stated: Purl.

Next RS row: [K4, k2tog] to end. *(60 sts)*

Next RS row: [K3, k2tog] to end. *(48 sts)*

Next RS row: [K2, k2tog] to end. *(36 sts)*

Next RS row: [K1, k2tog] to end. *(24 sts)*

Next RS row: [K2tog] to end. *(12 sts)*

Next row: [P2tog] to end. *(6 sts)*

Break yarn and thread through rem sts.

Antenna

Make 2

Using US 5 (3.75mm) DPNs, cast on 5 sts in A.

Work 12 rows using the i-cord technique (see page 124)

Break yarn, thread through rem sts, and secure.

to make up hat

Sew back seam of hat using mattress stitch (see page 125).

Oversew (see page 126) the antennae to the top of the hat, using the photograph as a guide.

Weave in all loose ends.

rabbit
sweater

I love this sweater's simple style, not to mention the beautiful 100% wool yarn that comes in this delicious shade of peach, and a whole host of other fabulous colors. I've chosen to make my rabbit dreamy and sleepy looking, but you could also embroider eyes using the techniques shown on other projects in this book to give your bunny a more wide-awake look, if you prefer it that way.

yarn

Cascade 220 Superwash (100% wool) light worsted (DK) yarn

    2 x 3½oz (100g) balls (218yd/200m) in shade 1940 Peach (A)

    1 x 3½oz (100g) balls (218yd/200m) in shade 910 Winter White (B)

A small amount of dark gray light worsted (DK) yarn

needles and equipment

US 6 (4mm) knitting needles
2 x stitch holders (or a stitch holder and spare needle)
Yarn sewing needle
Large-eyed embroidery needle

gauge (tension)

20 sts and 28 rows in stockinette (stocking) stitch to a 4-in (10-cm) square on US 6 (4mm) needles.

measurements

To fit an average 12–18 month (2–3 year) old toddler. The sweater is 21½(23) in (54.5(58.5)cm) around the chest. The sleeves measure 9¾(10¼)in (22(26)cm) from shoulder to wrist.

For more details on sizes and sizing, see page 114.

abbreviations

See page 126.

to make sweater

Front

Using A, cast on 16(18) sts; using B, cast on 24 sts; using A from center of ball, cast on 16(18) sts. (56(60) sts)

Keeping to the color patt set and beg with a k row, work 32(38) rows in st st.

Next row: K16(18) in A, k6 in B, k12 in A (from second ball), k6 in B, k in A to end.

Next row: P16(18) in A, p5 in B, p14 in A, p5 in B, p in A to end.

Keeping to the color patt set and beg with a k row, work 12(18) rows in st st.

Next row: K17(19) in A, k3 in B, k10 in A, k3 in B, k in A to end. Break B and cont in A.

Next row: Purl.

Next row: Bind (cast) off 3 sts, k to end. (53(57) sts)

Next row: Bind (cast) off 3 sts pwise, p to end. (50(54) sts)

Next row: K2, k2tog, k to last 4 sts, ssk, k2. (48(52) sts)

Next row: Purl.

Rep last 2 rows 7(9) times more. (34 sts)

Next row: K2, k2tog, k3, ssk, k1. Put rem sts on holder, turn, and cont on 8 sts just worked only.

*Next and every WS row: Purl.

Next RS row: K2, k2tog, k1, ssk, k1. (6 sts)

Next RS row: K1, k2tog, ssk, k1 (4 sts)

Next RS row: K2tog, ssk. (2 sts)

Next RS row: K2tog. (1 st)

(Do not work purl row.)

Fasten off.

With RS of work facing, put 10 outer sts from st holder onto needle so you are ready to work them on RS, leaving rem sts on holder.

Next row: K1, k2tog, k3, ssk, k2. (8 sts)

Work as for first side from * to end.

Back

Using A, cast on 56(60) sts.

Beg with a k row, work 48(60) rows in st st.

Next row: Bind (cast) off 3 sts, k to end. (53(57) sts)

Next row: Bind (cast) off 3 sts pwise, p to end. (50(54) sts)

Next row: K2, k2tog, k to last 4 sts, ssk, k2. (48(52) sts)

Next row: Purl.

Rep last 2 rows 12(14) times more. (24 sts)

Leave sts on stitch holder or spare needle.

Sleeves

Make 2

Cast on 36(40) sts in A.

Beg with a k row, work 6(10) rows in st st.

Next row: K1, m1, k to last st, m1, k1. (38(42) sts)

Beg with a p row, work 7 rows in st st.

Rep last 8 rows, 3 times more. (44(48) sts)

Size 2–3 years only

Beg with a k row, work 4 rows in st st.

Both sizes

Next row: Bind (cast) off 3 sts, k to end. (41(45) sts)

Next row: Bind (cast) off 3 sts pwise, p to end. (38(42) sts)

Next row: K2, k2tog, k to last 4 sts, ssk, k2. (36(40) sts)

Next row: Purl.

Rep last 2 rows 12(14) times more. (12 sts)

Leave sts on stitch holder or spare needle.

Neck edge

With right sides of pieces facing, knit across 12 sts on first sleeve, pick up and k 8 sts down one side of front, knit 14 sts from stitch holder on front, pick up and k 8 sts up second side of front, knit 12 sts on second sleeve, knit across 24 sts from back. (78 sts)

Beg with a p row, work 5 rows in st st.

Bind (cast) off.

to make up

Join armhole sections of sleeves to front and back pieces and neckband using mattress stitch (see page 125). Join side and sleeve seams.

Fold back ¾in (2cm) around the lower edges and cuffs and slip stitch in place.

Using the photograph as a guide and dark gray yarn, embroider the eyes using chain stitch (see page 124) and the nose and mouth using straight stitches (see page 124).

Weave in all loose ends.

chapter 2

heads,
hands, and
tiny toes

piglet hat

Pigs and piglets are some of the cleanest and most peaceful animals on the planet, never mind the most appealing. So of course I had to include a piglet as part of this collection. While I can't guarantee the hat will encourage its wearer to adopt a piglet's best habits, it's sure to make its owner squeal with delight.

yarn

Sublime Natural Aran (100% wool) worsted (Aran) yarn
   A small amount of shade 423 Dilly (A)

Drops Air (70% alpaca, 23% nylon, 7% wool) worsted (Aran) yarn
   1 x 1¾oz (50g) ball (142yd/130m) in shade 08 Light Pink (B)

A very small amount of mid-gray light worsted (DK) yarn

needles and equipment

US 8 (5mm) knitting needles

US 7 (4.5mm) knitting needles

Yarn sewing needle

Large-eyed embroidery needle

gauge (tension)

17 sts and 22 rows in stockinette (stocking) stitch to a 4-in (10-cm) square in B on US 8 (5mm) needles.

measurements

To fit an average 3–6 month (9–12 month) old baby.

The hat has a 15(16½)in (38(42)cm) circumference including front curve.

For more details on sizes and sizing, see page 114.

abbreviations

See page 126.

to make hat

Main part
Using US 8 (5mm) needles, cast on 66(72) sts in A.
Row 1: Knit.
Break yarn and join in B.
Row 2: Knit.
Row 3: P24(26), WT.
Row 4: Knit.
Row 5: P25(27), WT.
Row 6: Knit.
Row 7: P26(28), WT.
Row 8: Knit.

Row 9: Purl across all sts.
Row 10: K24(26), WT.
Row 11: Purl.
Row 12: K25(27), WT.
Row 13: Purl.
Row 14: K26(28), WT.
Row 15: Purl.
Now work across all sts.
Beg with a k row, work 16 rows in st st.
Size 9–12 months only
Row 32: [K10, k2tog] to end. *(66 sts)*
Row 33: Purl.

Both sizes

Next row: [K9, k2tog] to end. *(60 sts)*
**Next and every WS row unless
otherwise stated:** Purl.
Next RS row: [K3, k2tog] to end. *(48 sts)*
Next RS row: [K2, k2tog] to end. *(36 sts)*
Next RS row: [K1, k2tog] to end. *(24 sts)*
Next RS row: [K2tog] to end. *(12 sts)*
Next row: [P2tog] to end. *(6 sts)*
Break yarn and thread through rem sts.

Ear

Make 4
Using US 7 (4.5mm) needles, cast on 8 sts
in B.
Beg with a k row, work 8 rows in st st.
Row 9: K1, ssk, k2, k2tog, k1. *(6 sts)*
Row 10: Purl.
Row 11: K1, ssk, k2tog, k1. *(4 sts)*
Row 12: [P2tog] twice. *(2 sts)*
Row 13: K2tog. *(1 st)*
Fasten off.

to make up

Sew back seam of hat using mattress stitch
(see page 125).

Place two ear pieces right sides together
and oversew (see page 126) along the
sides. Turn the right way out and slip stitch
the cast-on edges together. Make the other
ear in the same way. Oversew the ears in
position using the photo as a guide.

Using the gray yarn, work two lines of chain
stitch (see page 124) for the eyes and two
French knots (see page 124) for the nostrils.

Weave in all loose ends.

piglet hat **49**

koala
bootees

A super-fluffy gray yarn is the secret
ingredient behind these adorable
bootees, which will keep little feet super-
toasty while looking super-cool. As soon
as I saw and touched the yarn, I just
knew I had to make something koala for
this collection—and I hope you agree
that these fit the bill perfectly.

yarn and materials

Rico Essentials Soft Merino Aran
(100% wool)
    1 x 1¾oz (50g) ball (109yd/100m) in
    shade 027 Azure (A)

Drops Air (70% alpaca, 23% nylon, 7%
wool) worsted (Aran) yarn
    1 x 1¾oz (50g) ball (142yd/130m) in
    shade 04 Medium Grey (B)

A small amount of black light worsted
(DK) yarn

A very small amount of 100% polyester
toy filling

needles and equipment

US 8 (5mm) knitting needles

US 6 (4mm) knitting needles

Yarn sewing needle

Large-eyed embroidery needle

gauge (tension)

17 sts and 22 rows in stockinette
(stocking) stitch to a 4-in (10-cm) square
on US 8 (5mm) needles.

measurements

The bootees will fit an average 3–6
month (6–9 month) old baby.

The sole of the bootee is 3½(3¾)in
(9(9.5)cm) long.

For more details on sizes and sizing, see
page 114.

abbreviations

See page 126.

to make bootees

Main part

Make 2

Using US 8 (5mm) needles, cast on 26(28) sts in A.

Size 3–6 months only

Row 1: [K2, p2] to last 2 sts, k2.

Row 2: [P2, k2] to last 2 sts, p2.

Rep rows 1–2, 7 times more.

Size 6–9 months only

Row 1: [K2, p2] to end.

Row 2: [K2, p2] to end.

Rep rows 1–2, 7 times more.

Both sizes

Row 17: Purl.

Break A and join in B.

Beg with a k row, work 6 rows in st st.

Next row: K17(18), turn.

Next row: P8, turn.

Cont working on 8 sts just worked only, leaving rem sts on needle.

Beg with a k row, work 12(14) rows in st st.

Break yarn, rejoin it at base of top of bootee (the base of the rectangle just knitted) on RS of work.

Pick up and k 8(9) sts up side of bootee top, k8 sts from LH needle, pick up and k 8(9) sts down side of bootee top then k rem 9 (10) sts. *(42(46) sts)*

Knit 5 rows.

Shape sole

Row 1: [K2, k2tog, ssk, k9(11), k2tog, ssk, k2] twice. *(34(38) sts)*

Row 2: Knit.

Row 3: [K1, k2tog, ssk, k7(9), k2tog, ssk, k1] twice. *(26(30) sts)*

Row 4: Knit.

Row 5: [K2tog, ssk, k5(7), k2tog, ssk] twice. *(18(22) sts)*

Bind (cast) off.

Ear

Make 4 (2 for each bootee)

Using US 6 (4mm) needles, cast on 10 sts in B.

Beg with a p row, work 3 rows in st st.

Row 4: [K2tog] to end. *(5 sts)*

Break yarn and thread it through rem sts.

to make up

Sew back and sole seam using flat stitch (see page 126).

Fold the ear pieces in half with the right side on the inside and oversew the side seam, leaving the lower edge open. Turn the ears the right way out. Stuff very lightly and stitch in place on the bootee, using the photograph as a guide.

Using the black yarn, work a tiny coil of chain stitches (see page 124) for the eyes and a bigger coil for the nose.

Weave in all loose ends.

cat hairband

For a slightly understated cute-creature look, this easy-to-knit hairband is the perfect choice. I'm a big fan of marmalade cats, so I've opted for a shade of bright orange. But the yarn comes in a great range of natural and jewel-bright colors, so there's nothing to stop you whipping up a cluster of adorable hairbands to match every outfit.

yarn

Red Heart Heads Up (80% acrylic, 20% wool) bulky (chunky) yarn
    1 x 3½oz (100g) ball (106yd/97m) in
    Shade 00262 Tangelo

needles and equipment

US10½ (6.5mm) knitting needles

Yarn sewing needle

gauge (tension)

13 sts and 18 rows in stockinette (stocking) stitch to a 4-in (10-cm) square on US 10½ (6.5mm) needles.

measurements

To fit an average 18 month–
3 year old toddler.

The circumference of the hairband is 16in (41cm) unstretched. To make it smaller or larger, simply knit fewer rows or a few rows more.

abbreviations

See page 126.

to make hairband

Band

Cast on 10 sts.
Row 1: Knit.
Row 2: K2, p6, k2.
Rep rows 1–2, 35 times more—or until the band is the desired length.
Bind (cast) off.

Ear

Make 4
Cast on 10 sts.
Row 1: P2tog, p6, p2tog. *(8 sts)*
Row 2: Knit.
Row 3: P2tog, p4, p2tog. *(6 sts)*
Row 4: Knit.
Row 5: P2tog, p2, p2tog. *(4 sts)*
Row 6: Ssk, k2tog. *(2 sts)*
Row 7: P2tog. *(1 st)*
Fasten off.

to make up

Using mattress stitch (see page 125) sew the two short edges of the hairband together.

Place two ear pieces right sides together and oversew (see page 126) along the side edges, leaving the lower edges open. Turn the right way out. Make the second ear in the same way. Oversew the ears in place on the top of the hairband, along both the front and back of the lower edges of the ears to make sure they stand upright. The distance between the ears should be about 1in (2.5cm).

Weave in all loose ends.

fox cub hat

There's just something beautiful about foxes—their color for a start, but also their elegance and their knowing look. So of course I had to include a fox cub hat in this collection. The hat is knitted in a soft wool-mix yarn that comes in some lovely shades. So although I don't think you can really beat a red fox, you could always knit a gray fox hat for your own little cub should the fancy take you.

yarn

Lion Brand Wool Ease (80% acrylic, 20% wool) worsted (Aran) yarn

   1 x 3oz (85g) ball (196yd/180m) in shade 199 Pumpkin (A)
   1 x 3oz (85g) ball (196yd/180m) in shade 099 Fisherman (B)

A small amount of black light worsted (DK) yarn

needles and equipment

US 7 (4.5mm) knitting needles

Yarn sewing needle

Large-eyed embroidery needle

gauge (tension)

17 sts and 24 rows in stockinette (stocking) stitch to a 4-in (10-cm) square on US 7 (4.5mm) needles..

measurements

To fit an average 6–12 month old baby (18 month–3 year old toddler).

The hat has a 15(16½)in (38(42)cm) circumference.

For more details on sizes and sizing, see page 114.

abbreviations

See page 126.

to make hat

Main part

Before you begin, wind off a small ball (approx. 2yd/1.8m) of A. Cast on 66(72) sts in A from outside of main ball.

Row 1: [K1, p1] to end.
Row 2: [P1, k1] to end.
Rep rows 1–2 once more.
Row 5: Knit.
Join in B.
Row 6: P18(21) in A, p30 in B, p in A to end using yarn from center of ball.
Row 7: K18(21) in A, k30 in B, k in A to end.

Row 8: P18(21) in A, p30 in B, p in A to end.
Row 9: K18(21) in A, k13 in B, k4 in A using yarn from small ball, k13 in B using yarn from center of ball, k in A to end.
Row 10: P18(21) in A, p13 in B, p4 in A, p13 in B, p in A to end.
Row 11: K18(21) in A, k12 in B, k6 in A, k12 in B, k in A to end.
Row 12: P18(21) in A, p12 in B, p6 in A, p12 in B, p in A to end.
Rep rows 11–12 once more.
Row 15: K18(21) in A, k11 in B, k8 in A, k11 in B, k in A to end.
Row 16: P18(21) in A, p11 in B, p8 in A, p11 in B, p in A to end.
Rep rows 15–16 once more.
Row 19: K18(21) in A, k10 in B, k10 in A, k10 in B, k in A to end.
Row 20: P18(21) in A, p9 in B, p12 in A, p9 in B, p in A to end.

Row 21: K18(21) in A, k8 in B, k14 in A, k8 in B, k in A to end.

Row 22: P18(21) in A, p7 in B, p16 in A, p7 in B, p in A to end.

Break all yarns except leading A.

Beg with a k row, work 6 rows in st st.

Size 6–12 months only

Row 29: [K9, k2tog] to end. *(60 sts)*

Size 18 months–3 years only

Row 29: [K4, k2tog] to end. *(60 sts)*

Both sizes

Row 30: Purl.

Row 31: [K3, k2tog] to end. *(48 sts)*

Row 32: Purl.

Row 33: [K2, k2tog] to end. *(36 sts)*

Row 34: Purl.

Row 35: [K1, k2tog] to end. *(24 sts)*

Row 36: Purl.

Row 37: [K2tog] to end. *(12 sts)*

Row 38: [P2tog] to end. *(6 sts)*

Break yarn and thread through rem sts.

Ear

Make 4, 2 in A and 2 in B

Cast on 12 sts.

Row 1: Knit.

Row 2: Purl.

Row 3: K1, ssk, k to last 3 sts, k2tog, k1. *(10 sts)*

Beg with a p row, work 3 rows in st st.

Rep rows 3–6 (last 4 rows) once more. *(8 sts)*

Row 11: K1, ssk, k2, k2tog, k1. *(6 sts)*

Row 12: Purl.

Row 13: K1, ssk, k2tog, k1. *(4 sts)*

Row 14: [P2tog] twice. *(2 sts)*

Row 15: K2tog. *(1 st)*

Fasten off.

to make up

Sew back seam of hat using flat stitch (see page 126).

Place one ear piece in A and one in B right sides together. Oversew (see page 126) along the sides. Turn the right way out and slip stitch the cast-on edges together. Make the other ear in the same way. Oversew the ears in position using the photograph as a guide. Using A, work a row of chain stitch (see page 124) along the side seams of the ears.

Using the black yarn, work two lines of chain stitch for the eyes and a coil of chain stitch for the nose.

Weave in all loose ends.

mouse
mittens

Is it a mitten? Is it a glove puppet?
It's a little bit of both, of course.
These mousey mitts make it as
easy as pie to persuade little ones
to put on their gloves when the
mercury dips, so you won't hear
complaints about freezing little
fingers. I've chosen to knit these
mice in off-white — but I think little
mice in gray, or in pastel shades of
pink or blue, would be just as cute.
So take your pick.

yarn

Sublime Baby Cashmere Merino Silk
DK (75% merino wool, 20% silk, 5%
cashmere) light worsted (DK) yarn
    1 x 1¾oz (50g) ball (126yd/116m) in
    shade 346 Dusty Pink (A)
    1 x 1¾oz (50g) ball (126yd/116m) in
    shade 344 Little Linen (B)

A very small amount of black light
worsted (DK) yarn

needles and equipment

US 3 (3.25mm) knitting needles

US 6 (4mm) knitting needles

Yarn sewing needle

Large-eyed embroidery needle

gauge (tension)

22 sts and 28 rows in stockinette
(stocking) stitch to a 4-in (10-cm) square
on US 6 (4mm) needles.

measurements

To fit an average 12–18 month (2–3 year)
old toddler.

The palm of the mitten is 4(4½)in
(10(11.5)cm) from the top of the rib
section to the end of the mitten and is
4¾(5¼)in (12(13.5)cm) around hand.

For more details on sizes and sizing, see
page 114.

abbreviations

See page 126.

to make mittens

Right mitten

Using US 3 (3.25mm) needles and A, cast on 28(30) sts.

Size 12–18 months only

Row 1: [K2, p2] to end.

Row 2: [K2, p2] to end.

Rep rows 1–2, 4 times more.

Size 2–3 years only

Row 1: [K2, p2] to last 2 sts, k2.

Row 2: [P2, k2] to last 2 sts, p2.

Rep rows 1–2, 4 times more.

Both sizes

Break A, join in B and switch to US 6 (4mm) needles.

Beg with a k row, work 2 rows in st st.*

Row 13: K15(16), m1, k1, m1, k to end. *(30(32) sts)*

Row 14 and every WS row unless otherwise stated: Purl.

Row 15: K15(16), m1, k3, m1, k to end. *(32(34) sts)*

Row 17: K15(16), m1, k5, m1, k to end. *(34(36) sts)*

Row 19: K15(16), m1, k7, m1, k to end. *(36(38) sts)*

Row 21: K24(25), turn.

Row 22: P9, turn.

Beg with a k row, work 6 rows in st st on 9 sts just worked.

Next row: [Ssk] twice, k1, [k2tog] twice. *(5 sts)*

Break yarn and thread it through rem sts.

**With RS of work facing, put the last st on the RH needle (the st nearest the center) onto the LH needle. Rejoin yarn to sts on LH needle.

Next row: [Inc] twice, k to end.

Now work across all 29(31) sts.

Beg with a p row, work 13(17) rows in st st.

Next row: K2, ssk, k7(8), k2tog, k3, ssk, k7(8), k2tog, k2. *(25(27) sts)*

Next and every WS row unless otherwise stated: Purl.

Next RS row: K2, ssk, k5(6), k2tog, k3, ssk, k5(6), k2tog, k2. *(21(23) sts)*

Next RS row: [K2tog] 5(6) times, k3(1), [k2tog] 4(5) times. *(12 sts)*

Next row: [P2tog] 6 times. *(6 sts)*

Break yarn and thread through rem sts.

Left mitten

Work as for right mitten to *.

Row 13: K12(13), m1, k1, m1, k to end. *(30(32) sts)*

Row 14 and every WS row unless otherwise stated: Purl.

Row 15: K12(13), m1, k3, m1, k to end. *(32(34) sts)*

Row 17: K12(13), m1, k5, m1, k to end. *(34(36) sts)*

Row 19: K12(13), m1, k7, m1, k to end. *(36(38) sts)*

Row 21: K21(22), turn.

Row 22: P9, turn.

Beg with a k row, 6 rows in st st on 9 sts just worked.

Next row: [Ssk] twice, k1, [k2tog] twice. *(5 sts)*

Break yarn and thread it through rem sts.

Work as for right mitten from ** to end.

Ear

Make 4 (2 for each mitten)

Using US 3 (3.25mm) needles and B, cast on 4 sts.

Row 1: [Inc, k1] twice. *(6 sts)*

Beg with a p row, work 3 rows in st st.

Row 5: Ssk, k2, k2tog. *(4 sts)*

Row 6: [P2tog] twice. *(2 sts)*

Row 7: [Inc] twice. *(4 sts)*

Row 8: [Inc pwise, p1] twice. *(6 sts)*

Beg with a k row, work 3 rows in st st.

Row 12: P2tog, p2, p2tog. *(4 sts)*

Bind (cast) off.

to make up

Join thumb and mitten seams using mattress stitch (see page 125).

Fold ears so that the right sides are on the inside and oversew (see page 126) round curved edges, leaving the lower edges open. Turn the right way out and slip stitch the lower edge together, then pinch them in half and secure. Oversew in position using the photograph as a guide.

Using A, work a small coil of chain stitch (see page 124) for the nose. Using the black yarn, work two large French knots (see page 124) for the eyes.

Weave in all loose ends.

rabbit bootees

These soft pastel bunny bootees are guaranteed to keep little feet looking good as well as feeling cozy. The luxury yarn, which contains cashmere, is beautifully gentle on the skin—but is also machine washable. Bootees are much easier to knit than socks, and I reckon they're a great project to try if you've mastered simpler items like hats and feel like moving on.

yarn

Debbie Bliss Baby Cashmerino (55% wool, 33% acrylic, 12% cashmere) light worsted (DK) yarn

1 x 1¾oz (50g) ball (137yd/125m) in shade 094 Rose Pink (A)

1 x 1¾oz (50g) ball (137yd/125m) in shade 101 Ecru (B)

A small amount of black light worsted (DK) yarn

needles and equipment

US 7 (4.5mm) knitting needles

Yarn sewing needle

Large-eyed embroidery needle

gauge (tension)

18 sts and 26 rows in stockinette (stocking) stitch to a 4-in (10-cm) square on US 7 (4.5mm) needles with yarn used double.

measurements

To fit an average 0–6 month (6–12 month) old baby. Length of sole is 3¼(3¾)in (8.25(9.5)cm).

For more details on sizes and sizing, see page 114.

abbreviations

See page 126.

to make bootees

Main part

Make 2

Using A double, cast on 28(30) sts.

Row 1: K0(2), [p2, k2] to end.

Row 2: [P2, k2] to last 0(2) sts, p0(2).

Rep rows 1–2, 5 times more.

Row 13: K19(20), turn.

Row 14: P10, turn.

Beg with a k row, work 12(14) rows in st st.

Break yarn.

With RS facing, rejoin yarn to base of rectangle just worked.

Pick up and k 7(8) sts up first side, k across 10 sts on needle, pick up and k 7(8) sts down second side, k rem 9(10) sts. *(42(46) sts)*

Beg with a p row, work 3 rows in st st.

Next row: K3, k2tog, k to last 5 sts, ssk, k3. *(40(44) sts)*

Next row: Knit.

Break A and join in B, using it double.

Rep last 2 rows once more. *(38(42) sts)*

Next row: K3, k2tog, k10(12), ssk, k4, k2tog, k10(12), ssk, k3. *(34(38) sts)*

Next row: Knit.

Next row: K3, k2tog, k8(10), ssk, k4, k2tog, k8(10), ssk, k3. *(30(34) sts)*

Next row: Knit.

Next row: K3, k2tog, k6(8), ssk, k4, k2tog, k6(8), ssk, k3. *(26(30) sts)*

Next row: Knit.

Bind (cast) off.

Ear

Make 4 (2 for each bootee)

Using A double, cast on 3 sts.

Knit 16 rows.

Row 17: Sl1, k2tog, psso. *(1 st)*

Fasten off.

to make up

Sew back and sole seam using flat stitch (see page 126).

Oversew the ears in position using the photograph as a guide.

Using the black yarn, work two small circles of chain stitches (see page 124) or French knots (see page 124) for the eyes. Work the nose and mouth in straight stitch (see page 124) using the photograph as a guide.

Weave in all loose ends.

big bear hat

When it's seriously cold outside, a big wooly hat is the perfect solution. This bear balaclava is designed to fit quite loosely, so it's really comfortable and easy to wear, and will fit a range of ages. And because it's knitted in a super-thick yarn, the hat is one of the quickest projects to knit in this book and, even though I say so myself, one of the most satisfying. As well as a range of lovely naturals, this wool-rich yarn comes in a selection of beautiful soft colors.

yarn

Red Heart Grande (78% acrylic, 22% wool) super-bulky (super-chunky) yarn
  2 x 5⅓oz (150g) balls (45yd/42m) in shade 00110 Aran (A)
  1 x 5⅓oz (150g) ball (45yd/42m) in shade 00307 Oatmeal (B)

A very small amount of black light worsted (DK) yarn

needles and equipment

US 19 (15mm) knitting needles

US 17 (13mm) knitting needles

Yarn sewing needle

gauge (tension)

6 sts and 8 rows in stockinette (stocking) stitch to a 4-in (10-cm) square on US 19 (15mm) needles.

measurements

The hat is designed to fit loosely and will fit most 2–3 year olds. The neck circumference is 27in (68.5cm) and the opening for the face is 21¼in (54cm).

abbreviations

See page 126.

to make hat

Head

Using US 19 (15mm) needles, cast on 28 sts in A.
Beg with a k row, work 14 rows in st st.
Row 15: K10, ssk, k4, k2tog, k to end. *(26 sts)*
Row 16: Purl.
Row 17: K10, ssk, k2, k2tog, k to end. *(24 sts)*
Bind (cast) off pwise.

Neck

Using US 19 (15mm) needles and A, with RS facing and
starting from cast-on edge, pick up and k 18 sts along side
to bound- (cast-) off edge, then pick up and k another 18 sts
down second side from bound- (cast-) off edge to cast-on
edge. *(36 sts)*
Turn work and cast on 6 sts*. *(42 sts)*
Beg with a p row, work 9 rows in st st.
Break A and join in B.
Knit 2 rows.
Bind (cast) off.

Face trim

Using US 19 (15mm) needles and B, with RS facing pick up
and k 6 sts along flap (formed from the 6 sts cast on at *) and
another 26 sts along the original cast-on edge of the main
part of hat. *(32 sts)*
Next row: Knit.
Bind (cast) off.

Ear

Make 4
Using US 17 (13mm) needles and A, cast on 6 sts.
Beg with a k row, work 4 rows in st st.
Row 5: Ssk, k2, k2tog. *(4 sts)*
Row 6: [P2tog] twice. *(2 sts)*
Row 7: Ssk. *(1 st)*
Fasten off.

to make up

Join the seam at the back of the head and the neck seam
using mattress stitch (see page 125).

Place two ear pieces right sides together and oversew (see
page 126) round the curved edges. Turn right way out and
slip stitch the cast-on edges together. Make the other ear
in the same way. Oversew the ears in position using the
photograph as a guide.

Weave in all loose ends.

chick socks

Perfect for Easter and for any other time of year, these socks are knitted in a hardwearing wool mix and one of my favorite yarns. If you're new to sock knitting, this is a pretty straightforward pattern; and many knitters say that once they start knitting socks, they often find themselves addicted. If you want to ring the changes, knit the socks in blue for a bluebird, green for a parrot—or keep it safe and go natural.

yarn

Sirdar Country Style DK (40% nylon, 30% wool, 30% acrylic) light worsted (DK) yarn 1 x 1¾oz (50g) ball (170yd/150m) in shade 629 Summer Blossom

Very small amounts of dark gray and orange light worsted (DK) yarn

needles and equipment

A set of four US 6 (4mm) double-pointed needles

US 6 (4mm) standard knitting needles (optional)

Stitch marker or small safety pin

Yarn sewing needle

Large-eyed embroidery needle

gauge (tension)

22 sts and 28 rows in stockinette (stocking) stitch to a 4-in (10-cm) square on US 6 (4mm) needles.

measurements

To fit an average 12–18 month (18 month–2 year) old toddler. The length of the socks from heel to toe is 4¼(5)in (11(12.5)cm).

abbreviations

See page 126.

to make socks

Sock

Make 2

Cast on 28(32) sts.

Divide the sts between 3 of the 4 double-pointed needles and k into the first cast-on st to form a circle. Place the stitch marker in this st to mark the first st of the round.

Rounds 1–5: [K1, p1] to end.

Rounds 6–16: Knit.

Round 17: K12(14), p4, k12(14).

Round 18: Knit.

Round 19: K11(13), p6, k11(13).

Round 20: Knit.

Round 21: K10(12), p8, k10(12).

Round 22: Knit.

Round 23: K9(11), p10, k9(11).

Round 24: Knit.

Rep rounds 23–24 twice more.

Heel flap

Row 29: K7(8), turn.

Row 30: P14(16). *(14(16) sts)*

Rearrange work so these 14(16) sts are all on one needle and work on these sts only.

Beg with a k row, work 10(12) rows in st st.

Next row: K9(11), ssk, k1, turn.

Next row: Sl1 pwise, p5(7), p2tog, p1, turn.

Next row: Sl1, k6(8), ssk, k1, turn.

Next row: Sl1 pwise, p7(9), p2tog, p1, turn. *(10(12) sts)*

Foot

Next row: Knit 10(12) sts. Put stitch marker on running bar between 5th and 6th (6th and 7th) sts of sts just knitted. With RS facing, pick up and k 6(7) sts up side of heel flap, turn work, p16(19) then pick up and p 6(7) sts up second side of heel flap. *(36(42) sts)*

Turn work and k up to and including st before marker. The main part of the foot is now worked in rounds from this point.

Round 1: K8(10), k2tog, k16(18), ssk, k8(10). *(34(40) sts)*

Round 2: Knit.

Round 3: K7(9), k2tog, k16(18), ssk, k7(9). *(32(38) sts)*

Round 4: Knit.

Round 5: K6(8), k2tog, k16(18), ssk, k6(8). *(30(36) sts)*

Round 6: Knit.

Round 7: K5(7), k2tog, k16(18), ssk, k5(7). *(28(34) sts)*

Round 8: Knit.

Round 9: K4(6), k2tog, k16(18), ssk, k4(6). *(26(32) sts)*

Round 10: Knit.

Round 11: K3(5), k2tog, k16(18), ssk, k3(5). *(24(30) sts)*

Rounds 12–20: Knit.

Round 21: K3(5), ssk, k2, k2tog, k6(8), ssk, k2, k2tog, k3(5). *(20(26) sts)*

Round 22: Knit.

Round 23: K2(4), ssk, k2, k2tog, k4(6), ssk, k2, k2tog, k2(4). *(16(22) sts)*

Size 18 months–2 years only

Round 24: Knit.

Round 25: K3, ssk, k2, k2tog, k4, ssk, k2, k2tog, k3. *(18 sts)*

Round 26: Knit.

Round 27: K2, ssk, k2, k2tog, k2, ssk, k2, k2tog, k2. *(14 sts)*

Both sizes

Break yarn, thread through rem sts, pull tightly, and secure.

Wing

Make 4 (2 for each sock)

Cast on 6 sts on standard needles (use two of the DPNs if you don't have standard needles).

Knit 6 rows.

Row 7: K1, k2tog, ssk, k1. *(4 sts)*

Row 8: Knit.

Row 9: K2tog, ssk. *(2 sts)*

Row 10: K2tog. *(1 st)*

Fasten off.

to make up

Oversew (see page 126) the wings in place on the side of the socks.

Using dark gray yarn, work a few chain stitches (see page 124) in a flattened U-shape for the eyes. Work a few vertical straight stitches (see page 124) in orange for the beak, then work a horizontal straight stitch at the base.

Weave in all loose ends.

chunky bunny hat

Who can resist a bunny hat, especially one as striking and straightforward to knit as this? Well not us, that's for certain. What's more, the hat is knitted in a gorgeously soft 100% acrylic yarn, so it's suitable for even the most sensitive skins. Because It's knitted on chunky needles, you'll also find your hat comes together really quickly—and who doesn't like that?

yarn

Lion Brand Hometown USA (100% acrylic) super-bulky (super-chunky) yarn
- 1 x 5oz (142g) ball (80yd/74m) in shade 194 Monterey Lime (A)
- 1 x 5oz (142g) ball (80yd/74m) in shade 102 Honolulu Pink (B)

needles and equipment

Size US 13 (9mm) knitting needles

Yarn sewing needle

gauge (tension)

9 sts and 12 rows in stockinette (stocking) stitch to a 4-in (10-cm) square on US 13 (9mm) needles.

measurements

The hat is designed to be worn slightly loosely and will fit most 2–3 year olds.

The neck circumference is 22in (56cm) and the opening for the face is 22in (56cm).

For more details on sizes and sizing, see page 114.

abbreviations

See page 126.

to make hat

Main part
Cast on 44 sts in A.
Beg with a k row, work 18 rows in st st.
Row 19: K17, ssk, k6, k2tog, k to end. *(42 sts)*
Row 20: Purl.
Row 21: K17, ssk, k4, k2tog, k to end. *(40 sts)*
Row 22: Purl.
Row 23: K17, ssk, k2, k2tog, k to end. *(38 sts)*
Bind (cast) off pwise.

Neck
With RS facing and using A and starting from cast-on edge, pick up and k 23 sts along side to bound- (cast-) off edge, then pick up and k another 23 sts down second side from bound- (cast-) off to cast-on edge. *(46 sts)*
Turn work and cast on 8 sts*. *(54 sts)*
Beg with a p row, work 3 rows in st st.
Break A and join in B.
Beg with a k row, work 2 rows in st st.
Knit 2 rows.
Bind (cast) off.

Face trim
With RS facing and using A, pick up and k 8 sts along flap (formed from the 8 sts cast on at *) and another 42 sts along the original cast-on edge of the main part of hat.
Next row: Knit.
Bind (cast) off.

Ear
Make 2
Cast on 9 sts in B.
Beg with a k row, work 24 rows in st st.
Break yarn and thread through sts.

to make up

Join the seam at the back of the head and the neck seam using mattress stitch (see page 125).

Join the long seam of the ears using mattress stitch. Oversew (see page 126) the ears in position using the photograph as a guide.

Weave in all loose ends.

hedgehog bootees

With a snug ribbed edging to make sure they stay put, these bootees are perfectly understated and will complement all manner of cool-season outfits. I love the real hedgehog colors used here, but the 100% wool yarn comes in a rainbow of tempting shades—so if you want to go "off piste," that could be a very good idea. Peony pink hedgehog bootees anyone?

yarn

Cascade 220 Heathers (100% wool) worsted (Aran) yarn

　1 x 3½oz (100g) ball (218yd/200m) in shade 2440 Vinci (A)

A small amount of cream or pale beige worsted (Aran) yarn (B)

A very small amount of black light worsted (DK) yarn

needles and equipment

US 6 (4mm) knitting needles

Yarn sewing needle

Large-eyed embroidery needle

gauge (tension)

20sts and 24 rows in stockinette (stocking) stitch to a 4-in (10-cm) square on US 6 (4mm) needles.

measurements

The hedgehog bootees will fit an average 3–6 month (6–9 month) old baby.

The sole of the bootie is 3½(3¾)in (9cm(9.5)cm) long.

For more details on sizes and sizing, see page 114.

abbreviations

See page 126.

to make bootees

Main part

Make 2

Cast on 26(30) sts in A.

Row 1: [K1, p1] to end.

Rep row 1, 9 times more.

Knit 6 rows.

Row 17: K17(19), turn.

Row 18: K8, turn and work on these 8 sts only to work top of bootee, leaving rem sts on needle.

Knit 12(16) rows.

Break A and join in B.

Beg with a k row, work 2 rows in st st.

Break B.

With RS facing and working up right-hand side of bootee top, pick up and knit 8(9) sts with A and 1 st with B.

Cont in B and k across 8 sts on needle and pick up and knit 1 st down left-hand side, then with A (from center of ball), pick up and knit 8(9) sts down left-hand side and knit 9(11) sts on needle. *(44(50) sts)*

Next row: K17(20) in A, p10 in B, k in A to end.

Next row: K17(20) in A, k10 in B, k in A to end.

Next row: K17(20) in A, p10 in B, k in A to end.

Next row: K17(20) in A, (k3, ssk, k2tog, k3) in B, k to end in A. *(42(48) sts)*

Next row: K17(20) in A, p8 in B, k in A to end.

Cont in A only.

Knit 2 rows.

Work sole

Next row: [K2, k2tog, ssk, k9(12), k2tog, ssk, k2] twice. *(34(40) sts)*

Next row: Knit.

Next row: [K1, k2tog, ssk, k7(10), k2tog, ssk, k1] twice. *(26(32) sts)*

Next row: Knit.

Next row: [K2tog, ssk, k5(8), k2tog, ssk] twice. *(18(24) sts)*

Next row: Knit.

Bind (cast) off.

Face trim

Make 2 (1 for each bootee)

Cast on 3 sts in A.

*Bind (cast) off 2 sts, sl rem st from RH to LH needle.

Cast on 2 sts.**

Rep from * to ** 6(7) times more, to make 7(8) picots.

Bind (cast) off.

to make up

Sew back and sole seam using flat stitch (see page 126).

Oversew (see page 126) the face trim in position round the edge of the face.

Using black yarn, work two French knots (see page 124) for the eyes and a small coil of chain stitch (see page 124) for the nose.

Weave in all loose ends.

little lamb
mittens

There are times when you yearn for something totally classic. These simple fingerless mittens, created in a wool-rich yarn with a touch of mohair, fit the bill perfectly. I've chosen a pale gray for this little lamb's face, but if you want to ring the changes, I think they'd also look cute in cream, brown, or even black And if you want something slightly less classic, how about using different colors; maybe soft blue or sea green?

yarn

Rowan Kid Classic (70% wool, 20% mohair, 8% polyamide) worsted (Aran) yarn

    1 x 1¾oz (50g) ball (153yd/140m) in shade 828 Feather (A)

A small amount of worsted (Aran) yarn in pale gray (B)

A very small amount of black light worsted (DK) yarn

needles and equipment

US 7 (4.5mm) knitting needles

US 6 (4mm) knitting needles

US G-6 (4mm) crochet hook (or one of a similar size)

Yarn sewing needle

Large-eyed embroidery needle

gauge (tension)

20 sts and 22 rows in stockinette (stocking) stitch to a 4-in (10-cm) square on US 7 (4.5mm) needles.

measurements

To fit an average 0-3 month (3–6 month) old baby.

The mittens are 3¼(4)in (8.5(10)cm) long (with cuff folded up).

abbreviations

See page 126.

to make mittens

Main part
Make 2
Using US 7 (4.5mm) needles, cast on 20(22) sts in A.
Row 1: [K2, p2] to last 0(2) sts, k0(2).
Row 2: P0(2), [k2, p2] to end.
Rep rows 1–2, 5(7) times more.
Knit 12(14) rows.
Break A and join in B.
Beg with a k row, work 4 rows in st st.
Next row: K2, ssk, k3(4), k2tog, k2, ssk, k3(4), k2tog, k2. *(16(18) sts)*
Next row: P2tog, p to last 2 sts, p2tog. *(14(16) sts)*
Next row: K1, ssk, k1(2), k2tog, k2, ssk, k1(2), k2tog, k1. *(10(12) sts)*
Next row: [P2tog] to end. *(5(6) sts)*
Break yarn, thread through rem sts, and secure.

Ear
Make 4 (2 for each mitten)
Using US 6 (4mm) needles, cast on 3 sts in B.
Work 4 rows in st st.
Row 5: Sl1, k2tog, psso. *(1 st)*
Fasten off.

Top knot
Make 2 (1 for each mitten)
For the top knot, use the crochet hook and A to make a 4-in (10-cm) chain (see page 122).

to make up

Join main seam of mittens using flat stitch (see page 126), reversing seam on cuff to fold over.

Sew the ears in position using the photograph as a guide.

Using black yarn, work two French knots (see page 124) for the eyes and a "Y" shape for the nose.

Arrange the crochet chain into three loops and sew securely in the center of the top of the face section.

Weave in all loose ends.

chapter 3

for the
nursery

puppy
snuggle blanket

After bathing or just when the weather turns
a little chilly, every baby loves to snuggle up
inside something cute and cozy—and this
blanket with its puppy hood is an ideal option.
The wool-mix yarn is super quick to knit and
comes in a beautiful blossom pink as well as this
lovely blue—so go with a traditional baby shade
or explore the options and choose something
gender neutral.

yarn

Lion Brand Wool Ease Thick & Quick (80%
acrylic, 20% wool) super-bulky (super-
chunky) yarn
   3 x 6oz (170g) balls (106yd/97m) in
   shade 105 Glacier (A)

Lion Brand Wool Ease Chunky (80%
acrylic, 20% wool) bulky (chunky) yarn
   1 x 4 ⁹⁄₁₀oz (140g) ball (153yd/140m)
   in shade 107 Bluebell (B)

A small amount of black light worsted
(DK) yarn

needles and equipment

US 13 (9mm) knitting needles

US 8 (5mm) knitting needles

Yarn sewing needle

Large-eyed embroidery needle

gauge (tension)

9 sts and 12 rows in stockinette (stocking)
stitch to a 4-in (10-cm) square using A on
US 13 (9mm) needles.

measurements

The finished blanket measures approx.
26½ x 23¾in (67 x 60cm) and is suitable
for babies from around 3 months old.

abbreviations

See page 126.

to make blanket

Main part
Using US 13 (9mm) needles, cast on 55 sts in A.
Knit 4 rows.
Row 5: [K1, p2] to last st, k1.
Row 6: [P2, k1] to last st, p1.
Row 7: Knit.
Row 8: Purl.
Rep rows 5–8, 18 times more.
Knit 3 rows.
Bind (cast) off.

Face
Make 1
Using US 13 (9mm) needles, cast on 3 sts in A.
Row 1: Knit.
Row 2: Inc, k to end. *(4 sts)*
Rep row 2, 19 times more. *(23 sts)*
Row 22: Knit.
Row 23: Knit.
Row 24: Inc, k to last 2 sts, inc, k1. *(25 sts)*
Rep rows 22–24, 3 times more. *(31 sts)*
Knit 2 rows.
Bind (cast) off.

Ear
Make 2
Using US 8 (5mm) needles, cast on 5 sts in B.
Knit 16 rows.
Row 17: Ssk, k1, k2tog. *(3 sts)*
Bind (cast) off.

to make up

Join the two sides of the triangular face to
one corner of the blanket using flat stitch (see
page 126).

Using the black yarn, work two small coils of
chain stitch (see page 124) for the eyes and a
slightly bigger coil for the nose. Add a straight
stitch (see page 124) at the bottom of the nose.
Using B, work a circle of chain stitch around one
of the eyes.

Using the photograph as a guide, oversew the
ears in place (see page 126).

Weave in all loose ends.

fluffy bunny pillow

This fluffy bunny pillow with its pompom tail is the perfect choice if you want to add a touch of style and comfort to a favorite chair. The yarn is soft and light and has a beautiful marl effect. I've chosen a pretty heather pink color—but the yarn comes in some lovely shades of blue as well. You can use a pompom maker to make the tail, or do it the old-fashioned way with some circles cut from a sheet of card.

yarn and materials

Rowan Brushed Fleece (65% wool, 30% alpaca, 5% polyester) bulky (chunky) yarn
2 x 1¾oz (50g) balls (114yd/105m) in shade 266 Heather (A)
1 x 1¾oz (50g) ball (114yd/105m) in shade 251 Cove (B)

A small amount of fluffy gray yarn (I used Drops Air in shade 04 Medium Grey)

Pillow (cushion) pad measuring16 x 16in (41 x 41cm)

needles and equipment

US 10½ (7mm) knitting needles

Yarn sewing needle

A pompom maker for a 1½-in (4-cm) pompom, or four cardboard circles each measuring 1½in (4cm) in diameter with a ¾-in (2-cm) hole in the center

gauge (tension)

11½ sts and 16 rows in stockinette (stocking) stitch to a 4-in (10-cm) square on US 10½ (7mm) needles.

measurements

The cover is for a pillow (cushion) pad measuring 16 x 16in (41 x 41cm). The bunny motif is 5½in (14cm) high.

abbreviations

See page 126.

to make pillow

Back

Cast on 44 sts in A.
Beg with a k row, work 62 rows in st st.
Bind (cast) off.

Front

Cast on 44 sts in A.
Work 20 rows in st st.
Row 21: K17, join in B and work 1st row of chart, k17.
This row sets position of chart.
Work rows 22–42 in st st as set, completing motif from chart.
Break B and cont in A.
Beg with a k row, work 20 rows in st st.
Bind (cast) off.

to make up

Using the pompom maker or cardboard circles, make a pompom in gray yarn. Trim the pompom and use the tails of yarn to sew it in place for the bunny's tail.

Join pillow seams using mattress stitch (see page 125), inserting pad before sewing up final seam.

Weave in all loose ends.

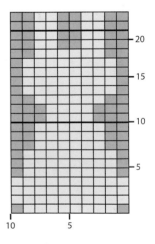

Key

⬛ Heather (A)
⬜ Cove (B)

hanging
birds

This delicate trio are knitted in a good-value yarn that comes in lots of baby-friendly shades. Because a bird uses such a small amount, they're a great way of using any small leftovers. I loved knitting them so much and they come together so quickly, I was tempted to knit a flock. I hope you love them too, and that you'll think up lots of ways to use them to decorate a baby's room.

yarn and materials

Cascade Cherub DK (55% nylon, 45% acrylic) light worsted (DK) yarn
 1 x 1¾oz (50g) ball (180yd/165m) in shade 13 Jade
 1 x 1¾oz (50g) ball (180yd/165m) in shade 15 Orchid
 1 x 1¾oz (50g) ball (180yd/165m) in shade 28 Boy Blue
 1 x 1¾oz (50g) ball (180yd/165m) in shade 17 Grey for the cord and tassel

Very small amounts of black and yellow light worsted (DK) yarns

A few handfuls of 100% polyester toy filling

needles and equipment

US 3 (3.25mm) knitting needles

US D-3 (3.25mm) crochet hook (or one of a similar size)

Yarn sewing needle

Large-eyed embroidery needle

gauge (tension)

25 sts and 34 rows in stockinette (stocking) stitch to a 4-in (10-cm) square on US 3 (3.25mm) needles.

measurements

Each bird measures 3½in (9cm) across.

abbreviations

See page 126.

Make three birds, one in each of the main colors.

to make bird

First side
Cast on 15 sts.
Row 1: Inc, k to last 2 sts, inc, k1. *(17 sts)*
Row 2: Purl.
Row 3: K1, m1, k to last st, m1, k1. *(19 sts)*
Row 4: Purl.
Rep rows 3–4, 3 times more.* *(25 sts)*
Beg with a k row, work 6 rows in st st.
Row 17: Bind (cast) off 14 sts, k to end. *(11 sts)*
Beg with a p row, work 5 rows in st st.
**Row 23: K1, k2tog, k to last 3 sts, ssk, k1. *(9 sts)*
Row 24: P2tog, p5, p2tog. *(7 sts)*
Row 25: K1, k2tog, k1, ssk, k1. *(5 sts)*
Bind (cast) off pwise.

Second side
Work as for first side to *.
Beg with a k row, work 5 rows in st st.
Row 16: Bind (cast) off 14 sts pwise, p to end. *(11 sts)*
Beg with a k row, work 6 rows in st st.
Work as for first side from ** to end.

Cords
Using the crochet hook and gray yarn, make four lengths of crochet chain (see page 122), one 8-in (20-cm) long chain for the top and three 3-in (8-cm) long chains. Leave tails of yarn at the start and end of each chain for sewing.

Tassel
Wrap gray yarn around four fingers approximately 20 times. Ease the yarn off fingers and cut the loops once to make a bundle of yarn lengths. Tie the yarn tail from one of the smaller chain lengths (see above) around the center of the lengths, so the chain butts right up to the lengths. Hold the chain so that the lengths hang downward. Tie a short length of gray yarn round the lengths, about ½in (1cm) down from the top of the tassel, tying it as tightly as possible. Trim the yarn loops to complete the tassel.

to make up

Place the two pieces for each bird right sides together. Oversew (see page 126) around the outer edge, leaving the lower edge open for turning and stuffing. Turn the piece right sides out. Stuff fairly lightly and close the lower edge using mattress stitch (see page 125).

Using the yarn double, embroider the wings in chain stitch (see page 124) using the photograph as a guide. Using black yarn, work French knots (see page 124) for the eyes. Using yellow yarn, work French knots for the beaks.

Join the birds together with the lengths of crochet chain, sewing the tails of yarn at the ends of the chains to the tops and bottoms of the birds. Make sure the long length is attached to the top bird and the tassel is at the bottom. Form the free end of the top length into a loop for hanging.

Weave in all loose ends.

owl storage baskets

These handy storage baskets not only look lovely, they'll also keep all your bits and pieces tidily stashed away, ready for when you need them. The owls are knitted in a simple seed (moss) stitch to create an interesting texture, and although I've chosen a robust citrus shade for mine, this gorgeous 100% natural yarn is available in a range of colors that would complement any nursery décor. Did I mention that the pattern includes baskets in two sizes?

yarn and materials

Debbie Bliss Roma (70% wool, 30% alpaca) super-bulky (super-chunky) yarn
   1 x 3½oz (100g) ball (87yd/80m) in shade 008 Citrus

Small amounts of dark gray and orange light worsted (DK) yarns

A very small amount of off-white light worsted (DK) yarn

2 x ½-in (12-mm) pale blue buttons for larger basket

2 x ⁵⁄₁₆-in (8-mm) pale blue buttons for smaller basket

Black sewing thread

A very small amount of 100% polyester toy filling

needles and equipment

US 15 (10mm) knitting needles

US 7 (4.5mm) knitting needles

Yarn sewing needle

Large-eyed embroidery needle

Standard sewing needle

gauge (tension)

10 sts and 13 rows in stockinette (stocking) stitch to a 4-in (10-cm) square on US 15 (10mm) needles.

measurements

The finished larger basket stands 6½in (16.5cm) tall and the smaller one 3½in (9cm) tall.

abbreviations

See page 126.

to make large basket

Body
Using US 15 (10mm) needles, cast on 34 sts.
Beg with a k row, work 4 rows in st st.
Row 5: [K1, p1] to end.
Row 6: [P1, k1] to end.
Rep rows 5–6, 12 times more.
Row 31: [K2tog] to end. *(17 sts)*
Row 32: Knit.
Row 33: K1, [k2tog] to end. *(9 sts)*
Row 34: Knit.
Break yarn and thread through rem sts.

Wing
Make 2
Using US 15 (10mm) needles, cast on 5 sts.
Row 1: [K1, p1] to last st, k1.
Rep row 1, 5 times more.
Row 7: P2tog, k1, p2tog. *(3 sts)*
Row 8: P1, k1, p1.
Row 9: Sl1, k2tog, psso. *(1 st)*
Fasten off.

Eye base
Make 2
Using dark gray yarn double and US 7 (4.5mm) needles,
cast on 20 sts.
Row 1: [K2tog] to end. *(10 sts)*
Row 2: [P2tog] to end. *(5 sts)*
Break yarn, thread through rem sts, and secure.

Beak
Using orange yarn double and US 7 (4.5mm) needles,
cast on 8 sts.
Beg with a k row, work 2 rows in st st.
Row 3: K1, ssk, k2, k2tog, k1. *(6 sts)*
Row 4: P2tog, p2, p2tog. *(4 sts)*
Break yarn and thread through rem sts, and secure.

to make small basket

Body
Using US 15 (10mm) needles, cast on 22 sts.
Beg with a k row, work 4 rows in st st.
Row 5: [K1, p1] to end.
Row 6: [P1, k1] to end.
Rep rows 5–6, 5 times more.
Row 17: [K2tog] to end. *(11 sts)*
Row 18: Knit.
Row 19: K1, [k2tog] to end. *(6 sts)*

Row 20: Knit.
Break yarn and thread through rem sts.

Wing
Make 2
Using US 15 (10mm) needles, cast on 3 sts.
Row 1: K1, p1, k1.
Rep row 1, 4 times more.
Row 6: Sl1, k2tog, psso. *(1 st)*
Fasten off.

Eye base
Make 2
Using dark gray yarn double and US 7 (4.5mm) needles,
cast on 16 sts.
Row 1: [K2tog] to end. *(8 sts)*
Row 2: [P2tog] to end. *(4 sts)*
Break yarn, thread through rem sts, and secure.

Beak
Using orange yarn double and US 7 (4.5mm) needles,
cast on 6 sts.
Beg with a k row, work 2 rows in st st.
Row 3: K1, ssk, k2tog, k1. *(4 sts)*
Break yarn and thread through rem sts, and secure.

to make up

Join the lower and back seam of basket using flat stitch (see page 126).

Oversew (see page 126) wings in position at the sides.

Oversew eye bases in position. Using off-white yarn, work 8-point stars on the eye bases of the larger basket and 6-point stars on the eye bases of the smaller basket, using the photograph as a guide. Sew the buttons in place using black thread.

Sew the long seam of the beak, leaving the lower edge open. Stuff very lightly and oversew the beak in place.

Weave in all loose ends.

lamb snuggle blanket

Comfort blankets are a great way to help babies settle, so here I'd like to introduce a blanket with all the traditional attributes, plus a bit more personality. I've knitted the main blanket in one of my favorite but oh-so-easy to work textures. And I've used a soft luxury yarn with a touch of cashmere that comes in a range of adorable shades—so check them out now and take your pick.

yarn and materials

Debbie Bliss Cashmerino Aran (55% wool, 33% acrylic, 12% cashmere) worsted (Aran) yarn

  1 x 1¾oz (50g) ball (98yd/90m) in
  shade 073 Coral (A)

Drops Air (70% alpaca, 23% nylon, 7% wool) worsted (Aran) yarn

  1 x 1¾oz (50g) ball (142yd/130m) in
  shade 01 Off White (B)

A small amount of light beige worsted (Aran) yarn (C)

A very small amount of black light worsted (DK) yarn

A few handfuls of polyester toy filling

needles and equipment

Size US 8 (5mm) knitting needles

Size US 7 (4.5mm) knitting needles

Size US 6 (4mm) knitting needles

Yarn sewing needle

Large-eyed embroidery needle

gauge (tension)

18 sts and 24 rows in stockinette (stocking) stitch to a 4-in (10-cm) square on US 8 (5mm) needles for A.

18 sts and 24 rows in stockinette (stocking) stitch to a 4-in (10-cm) square on US 7 (4.5mm) needles for B.

measurements

The blanket is approx. 10 x 10in (25 x 25cm).

It is safe for children from birth onward, so long as all parts are very firmly secured.

abbreviations

See page 126.

Row 19: Purl.

Row 20: K2, [ssk] twice, sl2, k1, p2sso, k5, sl2, k1, p2sso, [k2tog] twice, k2. *(15 sts)*

Row 21: P2tog, p to last 2 sts, p2tog. *(13 sts)*

Row 22: K2, [ssk] twice, k1, [k2tog] twice, k2. *(9 sts)*

Break yarn, thread through rem sts, and secure.

Ear

Make 2

Using US 6 (4mm) needles, cast on 4 sts in B.

Knit 4 rows.

Row 5: Ssk, k2tog. *(2 sts)*

Row 6: K2tog. *(1 st)*

Fasten off.

Arm

Make 2

Using US 7 (4.5mm) needles, cast on 7 sts in B.

Beg with a k row, work 14 rows in st st.

Break yarn, join in C, and change to US 6 (4mm) needles.

Beg with a k row, work 3 rows in st st.

Row 18: P2tog, p3, p2tog. *(5 sts)*

Break yarn, thread through rem sts, and secure.

to make blanket

Blanket

Using US 8 (5mm) needles, cast on 40 sts in A.

Knit 4 rows.

Row 5: K4, [p2, k1] to last 3 sts, k3.

Row 6: K3, [p1, k2] to last 4 sts, p1, k3.

Row 7: Knit.

Row 8: K3, p to last 3 sts, k3.

Rep rows 5–8, 14 times more.

Rep rows 5–6 once more.

Knit 4 rows.

Bind (cast) off.

Head

Using US 7 (4.5mm) needles, cast on 7 sts in B.

Row 1: [Inc] to end. *(14 sts)*

Row 2: Knit.

Row 3: [K2, m1] to last 2 sts, k2. *(20 sts)*

Row 4: Knit.

Rep rows 3–4 once more. *(29 sts)*

Knit 5 rows.

Break yarn, join in C, and change to US 6 (4mm) needles.

Beg with a k row, work 6 rows in st st.

Row 18: K2, ssk, k4, sl2, k1, p2sso, k7, sl2, k1, p2sso, k4, k2tog, k2. *(23 sts)*

to make up

Fold the head piece in half so the right side is on the outside and the row ends meet. Join this seam using flat stitch (see page 126), leaving the cast-on edge open for stuffing. Stuff head fairly firmly and close gap.

Sew the ears in place.

Using black yarn, work two French knots (see page 124) for the eyes and a "Y" shape in straight stitch (see page 124) for the nose.

Sew the long seam of the arms using mattress stitch (see page 125) and matching yarns, leaving the short edge open. Stuff lightly. Stitch the cast-on edge of the arms in place on the center of the blanket, so they point to opposite corners.

Sew the head in place.

Weave in all loose ends.

penguin toy

While teddies and toy rabbits are lovely, I wanted to do something a little different, so that's why I created this endearing penguin, complete with wooly scarf to keep out the seasonal chills. Because his eyes are embroidered he's completely safe for babies—but make sure you remove his scarf first and double-check that all the small parts are very securely stitched on.

yarn and materials

Lion Brand Wool Ease (80% acrylic, 20% wool) worsted (Aran) yarn

- 1 x 3oz (80g) ball (196yd/180m) in shade 099 Fisherman (A)
- 1 x 3oz (80g) ball (196yd/180m) in shade 153 Black (B)

A small amount of bright yellow light worsted (DK) yarn (C)

A small amount of light worsted (DK) yarn in color of your choice for scarf (D)

Approx. 1oz (just over 25g) 100% polyester toy filling

needles and equipment

US 6 (4mm) knitting needles

US 3 (3.25mm) knitting needles

US 5 (3.75mm) needles

Yarn sewing needle

Large-eyed embroidery needle

gauge (tension)

18 sts and 26 rows in stockinette (stocking) stitch to a 4-in (10-cm) square on US 6 (4mm) needles.

measurements

The penguin toy is 7in (18cm) tall.

abbreviations

See page 126.

to make penguin

Body front

Using US 6 (4mm) needles, cast on 12 sts in A.

Row 1: Inc, k to last 2 sts, inc, k1. *(14 sts)*

Row 2: Purl.

Row 3: K1, m1, k to last st, m1, k1. *(16 sts)*

Row 4: Purl.

Rep rows 3–4 once more. *(18 sts)*

Beg with a k row, work 22 rows in st st.

Row 29: K2, ssk, k to last 4 sts, k2tog, k2. *(16 sts)*

Row 30: Purl.

Rep row 29–30 once more. *(14 sts)*

Bind (cast) off.

Body back

Using US 6 (4mm) needles, cast on 12 sts in B.

Row 1: Inc, k to last 2 sts, inc, k1. *(14 sts)*

Row 2: Purl.

Row 3: K1, m1, k to last st, m1, k1. *(16 sts)*

Row 4: Purl.

Rep rows 3–4 twice more. *(20 sts)*

Beg with a k row, work 20 rows in st st.

Row 29: K2, ssk, k to last 4 sts, k2tog, k2. *(18 sts)*

Row 30: Purl.

Rep rows 29–30 once more. *(16 sts)*

Bind (cast) off.

Head front

Before you begin, wind off a separate 1yd (1m) length of B.

Using US 6 (4mm) needles, cast on 14 sts in A.

Row 1: Inc, k2, inc, k5, inc, k2, inc, k1. *(18 sts)*

Beg with a p row, work 5 rows in st st.

Row 7: K7 in A, k4 in B, k in A (from center of ball) to end.

Row 8: P6 in A, p6 in B (from wound-off length), p in A to end.

Row 9: K6 in A, k6 in B, k in A to end.

Row 10: P6 in A, p6 in B, p in A to end.

Row 11: K5 in A, k8 in B, k in A to end.

Row 12: P2 in B (from main ball), p2 in A, p10 in B, p2 in A, p2 in B (from center of ball).

Break all yarns except for leading B.

Beg with a k row, work 4 rows in st st.
Row 17: K2, [ssk] twice, k6, [k2tog] twice, k2. *(14 sts)*
Row 18: P2tog, p to last 2 sts, p2tog. *(12 sts)*
Bind (cast) off.

Head back

Using US 6 (4mm) needles, cast on 16 sts in B.
Row 1: Inc, k2, inc, k7, inc, k2, inc, k1. *(20 sts)*
Beg with a p row, work 15 rows in st st.
Row 17: K2, [ssk] 3 times, k4, [k2tog] 3 times, k2. *(14 sts)*
Row 18: P2tog, p to last 2 sts, p2tog. *(12 sts)*
Bind (cast) off.

Wing

Make 2
Using US 6 (4mm) needles, cast on 10 sts in B.
Beg with a k row, work 8 rows in st st.
Row 9: K1, ssk, k to last 3 sts, k2tog, k1. *(8 sts)*
Row 10: Purl.
Rep rows 9–10 once more. *(6 sts)*
Row 13: K1, ssk, k2tog, k1. *(4 sts)*
Row 14: [P2tog] twice. *(2 sts)*
Row 15: K2tog. *(1 st)*
Fasten off.

Beak

Using US 3 (3.25mm) needles, cast on 10 sts in C.
Beg with a k row, work 2 rows in st st.
Row 3: K2, k2tog, k2, ssk, k2. *(8 sts)*
Row 4: Purl.
Row 5: K1, k2tog, k2, ssk, k1. *(6 sts)*
Row 6: P2tog, p2, p2tog. *(4 sts)*
Break yarn and thread through rem sts.

Feet

Make 2
Using US 3 (3.25mm) needles, cast on 6 sts in C.
Beg with a k row, work 6 rows in st st.
Row 7: K2tog, [yo, k2tog] twice. *(5 sts)*
Beg with a p row, work 7 rows in st st.
Bind (cast) off.

Scarf

Using US 5 (3.75mm) needles, cast on 5 sts in D.
Knit 110 rows.
Bind (cast) off.

to make up

Weave in all loose ends.

Join the head front to the head back using mattress stitch (see page 125), leaving the lower edges open. Join the front and back body pieces in the same way, leaving the top edges open. Stuff the pieces and join together using mattress stitch, pulling the yarn quite tightly to create the penguin's neck.

Fold the wings in half lengthwise so that the right side is facing outward and slip stitch along the top and the long edge. Oversew (see page 126) in place, just to the front of the side seams.

Fold the beak in half so that the right side is facing outward. Oversew the long seam, stuff lightly, and oversew in place.

Fold the feet in half widthwise so that the "holes" along the middle form the toes. Oversew around the edges, then oversew in place on the underside of the penguin.

Using B, work two small coils of chain stitch (see page 124) for the eyes. Work a coil in A around the outside of each eye.

Tie scarf around neck.

lion pillow

I've always loved 1970s graphic images and they were my inspiration for this friendly-looking lion, whom I hope will make the perfect companion. I've chosen great lion colors, and he's knitted in a super-bulky (super-chunky) yarn, so he comes together much quicker than you'd think. If you want to knit him a girlfriend or wife, simply make another pillow and omit the mane.

yarn and materials

Lion Brand Hometown USA (100% acrylic) super-bulky (super-chunky) yarn
  2 x 5oz (142g) balls (80yd/74m) in shade 131 Atlanta Apricot (A)
  1 x 5oz (142g) ball (80yd/74m) in shade 170 Las Vegas Gold (B)

A small amount of super-bulky (super-chunky) black yarn (C)

A 16-in (40-cm) diameter round pillow (cushion) pad

needles and equipment

US 13 (9mm) knitting needles

Yarn sewing needle

Large-eyed embroidery needle

gauge (tension)

9 sts and 12 rows in stockinette (stocking) stitch to a 4-in (10-cm) square on US 13 (9mm) needles.

measurements

Cover will fit a 16-in (40-cm) diameter round pillow (cushion) pad.

abbreviations

See page 126.

to make pillow

Head

Make 2

Cast on 14 sts in A.

Row 1: Inc, k to last 2 sts, inc, k1. *(16 sts)*

Row 2: Purl.

Row 3: K2, m1, k to last 2 sts, m1, k2. *(18 sts)*

Row 4: Purl.

Rep rows 3–4, 8 times more. *(34 sts)*

Beg with a k row, work 14 rows in st st.

Row 35: K2, k2tog, k to last 4 sts, ssk, k2. *(32 sts)*

Row 36: Purl.

Rep rows 35–36, 8 times more. *(16 sts)*

Row 53: K2, k2tog, k to last 4 sts, ssk, k2. *(14 sts)*

Bind (cast) off pwise.

Mane

Cast on 2 sts in B.

Rows 1–3: Knit.

Row 4: Cast on 6 sts, bind (cast) off 6 sts, then k1. *(2 sts)*

Rep rows 1–4, 33 times more.

Bind (cast) off rem st and fasten off.

Ear

Make 2

Cast on 6 sts in A.

Beg with a k row, work 4 rows in st st.

Row 5: Ssk, k2, k2tog. *(4 sts)*

Row 6: [P2tog] twice. *(2 sts)*

Row 7: [Inc] twice. *(4 sts)*

Row 8: [Inc pwise, p1] twice. *(6 sts)*

Beg with a k row, work 3 rows in st st.

Bind (cast) off pwise.

Nose

Cast on 3 sts in B.

Beg with a k row, work 4 rows in st st.

Row 5: K1, [m1, k1] twice. *(5 sts)*

Beg with a p row, work 5 rows in st st.

Row 11: K1, m1, k3, m1, k1. *(7 sts)*

Beg with a p row, work 9 rows in st st.

Break A and join in C.

Beg with a k row, work 2 rows in st st.

Row 23: Ssk, k3, k2tog. *(5 sts)*

Row 24: Purl.

Row 25: Ssk, k1, k2tog. *(3 sts)*

Row 26: P3tog *(1 st)*

Fasten off.

to make up

Place the two face pieces wrong sides together and join the outside seam using mattress stitch (see page 125), leaving one side open to insert the pillow (cushion) pad. Insert the pad and continue in mattress stitch to close the gap.

Oversew (see page 126) the nose in place using matching yarns, following the photo as a guide. Using a separated strand of C, work the eyes and mouth in chain stitch (see page 124), again using the photograph as a guide.

Fold the ear pieces right sides together and oversew around the curved edge, leaving the lower edge open. Turn the right way out and sew in position.

Slip stitch the mane in place, just in front of the side seam.

Weave in all loose ends.

fish cocoon and hat

Knitted in a washable yarn that comes in a fabulous range of colors, this cocoon is the chic option for babies who want to keep cozy when there's a chill in the air, without sacrificing their sense of style. The cocoon is knitted in a decorative twist stitch that has just enough interest to keep you on your toes, without being too tricky. If you're new to fancy stitches, this is a great place to start.

yarn

Cascade Pacific Chunky (60% acrylic, 40% wool) bulky (chunky) yarn
  1 x 3½oz (100g) ball (120yd/110m) in shade 33 Cactus (A)
  2 x 3½oz (100g) balls (120yd/110m) in shade 23 Dusty Turquoise (B)

(This will be sufficient for both the cocoon and hat. If you are knitting the cocoon only, you will still need this quantity of yarn.)

needles and equipment

US 10½ (7mm) knitting needles

Stitch holder

Yarn sewing needle

gauge (tension)

12 sts and 14 rows in stockinette (stocking) stitch to a 4-in (10-cm) square on US 10½ (7mm) needles.

measurements

Both items will fit an average baby from 0–3 months.

The finished cocoon measures 22½in (57cm) from the top to the bottom of the tail.

The hat is 13½in (34cm) in circumference.

For safety reasons, the baby should be placed in the cocoon so that the top edge comes around the baby's body, under the armpits.

abbreviations

See page 126.

to make cocoon

Cast on 57 sts in A.

Beg with a k row, work 5 rows in st st.

Break A and join in B.

Row 6: Purl.

Row 7: P2, [sl1 pwise, k2, psso, p2] to end.

Row 8: K2, [p1, yo, p1, k2] to end.

Row 9: P2, [k3, p2] to end.

Row 10: K2, [p3, k2] to end.

Rep rows 7–10, 14 times more.

Row 67: P2tog, [sl1, k2tog, psso, p2tog] to end. *(23 sts)*

Row 68: Purl.

Row 69: K1, inc, k to end. *(24 sts)*

Row 70: P12, put rem 12 sts on holder and work on 12 sts on needle only.

***Next row:** K2, m1, k to last 2 sts, m1, k2. *(14 sts)*

Next row: Purl.

Rep last 2 rows, 5 times more. *(24 sts)*

Beg with a k row, work 4 rows in st st.

Break B and join in A.

Beg with a k row, work 2 rows in st st.

Bind (cast) off.

Put sts from stitch holder onto needle and rejoin B to WS of work.

Next row: Purl.

Rep from * to end.

to make hat

Cast on 42 sts in A.

Beg with a k row, work 20 rows in st st.

Row 21: K2, [sl2, k1, p2sso, k4] 5 times, sl2, k1, p2sso, k2. *(30 sts)*

Row 22: Purl.

Row 23: K1, [sl2, k1, p2sso, k2] 5 times, sl2, k1, p2sso, k1. *(18 sts)*

Row 24: Purl.

Row 25: [Sl2, k1, p2sso] 6 times. *(6 sts)*

Break yarn, thread through rem sts, pull up, and secure.

to make up

For cocoon, place two tail fin pieces right sides together and oversew (see page 126) around the sides and lower edge.

Turn the cocoon the right way out and sew the side seam using mattress stitch (see page 125).

Sew the back seam of the hat using mattress stitch.

Weave in all loose ends.

polar bear rug

If you want to add a bit of explorer chic to a nursery or playroom, you've landed on the right page. This polar bear rug is knitted in a sumptuous alpaca-rich yarn and it makes the perfect place for a baby or toddler to lie and chill. Because the yarn is super thick, it will knit up much quicker than you might think.

yarn and materials

Cascade Salar (50% alpaca, 45% acrylic, 5% wool) super-bulky (super-chunky) yarn

> 3 x 7oz (200g) balls (196yd/180m) in shade 07 White

Small amount of black light worsted (DK) yarn

A few handfuls of 100% polyester toy filling

1½yd (1.25m) of 59-in (150-cm) wide polyester fleece fabric in cream

Cream sewing thread

needles and equipment

US 13 (9mm) knitting needles

Stitch holder

2 x stitch markers or small safety pins

US M-13 (9mm) crochet hook

Water-soluble pen or quilters' pencil

Yarn sewing needle

Large-eyed embroidery needle

Standard sewing needle

Some pins

gauge (tension)

10 sts and 13 rows in stockinette (stocking) stitch to a 4-in (10-cm) square on US 13 (9mm) needles.

measurements

The rug is 45in (114cm) long from back foot to nose.

abbreviations

See page 126.

---

to make rug

First back leg

Cast on 8 sts.

Row 1: Inc, k to last 2 sts, inc, k1. *(10 sts)*

Row 2: Purl.

Rep rows 1–2 twice more. *(14 sts)*

Row 7: K2, m1, k to end. *(15 sts)*

Row 8: Purl.

Row 9: K2, m1, k to last 2 sts, m1, k2. *(17 sts)*

Row 10: Purl.

Rep rows 7–10 once more. *(20 sts)*

Row 15: K2, m1, k to last 4 sts, ssk, k2.

Row 16: Purl.

Rep rows 15–16 twice more.

Row 21: K2, m1, k to last 4 sts, ssk, k2.

Row 22: Purl.

Rep rows 21–22 twice more.

Break yarn and put sts on stitch holder.

Second back leg

Cast on 8 sts on needle with sts.

Row 1: Inc, k to last 2 sts, inc, k1. *(10 sts)*

Row 2: Purl.

Rep rows 1–2 twice more. *(14 sts)*

Row 7: K to last 2 sts, m1, k2. *(15 sts)*

Row 8: Purl.

Row 9: K2, m1, k to last 2 sts, m1, k2. *(17 sts)*

Row 10: Purl.

Rep rows 7–10 once more. *(20 sts)*

Row 15: K2, k2tog, k to last 2 sts, m1, k2.

Row 16: Purl.

Rep rows 15–16 twice more.

Row 21: K2, k2tog, k to last 2 sts, m1, k2.

Row 22: Purl.

Rep rows 21–22 twice more.

Leave sts on needle and do not break yarn.

Body and front legs

Row 27: K20 across second back leg, turn and cast on 20 sts, turn back and k20 from stitch holder. *(60 sts)*

Row 28: Purl.

Row 29: K2, k2tog, k to last 4 sts, ssk, k2. *(58 sts)*

Beg with a p row, work 9 rows in st st.

Rep rows 29–38 (last 10 rows) 3 times more. *(52 sts)*

Row 69: K2, m1, k to last 2 sts, m1, k2. *(54 sts)*

Row 70: Purl.

Rep rows 69–70, 4 times more. *(62 sts)*

Row 79: Cast on 6 sts, k to end. *(68 sts)*

Row 80: Cast on 6 sts, p to end. *(74 sts)*

Rep rows 79–80 once more. *(86 sts)*

Row 83: Cast on 4 sts, k to end. *(90 sts)*

Row 84: Cast on 4 sts, p to end. *(94 sts)*

Row 85: K2, m1, k to last 2 sts, m1, k2. *(96 sts)*

Row 86: Purl.

Rep rows 85–86 once more. *(98 sts)*

Beg with a k row, work 4 rows in st st.

Row 93: K2, k2tog, k to last 4 sts, ssk, k2. *(96 sts)*

Row 94: Purl.

Rep rows 93–94 once more. *(94 sts)*

Row 97: Bind (cast) off 4 sts, k to end. *(90 sts)*

Row 98: Bind (cast) off 4 sts pwise, p to end. *(86 sts)*

Row 99: Bind (cast) off 6 sts, k to end. *(80 sts)*

Row 100: Bind (cast) off 6 sts pwise, p to end. *(74 sts)*

Rep rows 99–100 once more. *(62 sts)*

Row 103: Bind (cast) off 5 sts, k to end. *(57 sts)*

Row 104: Bind (cast) off 5 sts pwise, p to end. *(52 sts)*

Rep rows 103–104 once more. *(42 sts)*

Row 107: Bind (cast) off 3 sts, k to end. *(39 sts)*
Row 108: Bind (cast) off 3 sts pwise, p to end. *(36 sts)*
Mark both ends of last row with a stitch marker or small safety pin.
*Row 109: K2, k2tog, k to last 4 sts, ssk, k2. *(34 sts)*
Row 110: Purl.
Rep rows 109–110, 6 times more. *(22 sts)*
Beg with a k row, work 10 rows in st st.
Row 133: K2, k2tog, k to last 4 sts, ssk, k2. *(20 sts)*
Row 134: P2, p2tog, p to last 4 sts, p2tog tbl, p2. *(18 sts)*
Rep rows 133–134 twice more. *(10 sts)*
Bind (cast) off.

Head underside
Cast on 36 sts and work from * to end of main piece.

Ear
Make 4
Cast on 4 sts.
Row 1: [Inc, k1] twice. *(6 sts)*
Row 2: Purl.
Row 3: K1, m1, k4, m1, k1. *(8 sts)*
Beg with a p row, work 3 rows in st st.
Row 7: Ssk, k4, k2tog. *(6 sts)*
Row 8: P2tog, p2, p2tog tbl *(4 sts)*
Row 9: Ssk, k2tog. *(2 sts)*
Row 10: P2tog. *(1 st)*
Fasten off.

to make up
Using the crochet hook, work a crochet edging (see page 122) around bear shape, excluding head (from stitch markers to end).

Using black yarn, work coils of chain stitch (see page 124) for the eyes and nose, using the photograph as a guide.

Place head underside piece on head part of main shape so that the right sides are together and the lower edge of the head underside piece matches up with the stitch markers. Oversew around the sides, leaving the cast-on edge open. Turn the head the right way out so the small head piece is now on the underside of the rug. Stuff very lightly then slip stitch the cast on edge in place.

Lay the knitted shape on cream fleece and draw around it, excluding the head part, with the water-soluble pen or quilters' pencil. Cut shape out. Pin the fleece fabric in place on the underside of the rug, with the right side of the fabric facing outward. Tuck the raw edge of the fleece under and slip stitch in place around the outer edges of the rug, just inside the crochet edge, and across the straight edge of the head piece.

Place two of the ear pieces right sides together and oversew (see page 126) around the curved edges, leaving the cast-on edge open for turning. Repeat for the second ear. Turn the ears the right way out and sew them in place, using the photograph as a guide. Pinch the two sides of the ear together at the lower edge and secure with a couple of stitches.

Weave in all loose ends.

whale pillow

Who doesn't love a smiling whale? Knitted in a fabulous deep blue in a quick-to-knit yarn, this is possibly my favorite project in this book and also one of the easiest, once you've learned how to "wrap and turn" (WT)—or "work short rows" as it's sometimes called (see Abbreviations on page 126 for instructions). The pillow uses a widely available pillow pad and the only other things you will need are a couple of buttons for the eyes, a contrasting yarn for the mouth, and a few handfuls of polyester toy filling. So what are you waiting for?

yarn and materials

Cascade Pacific Chunky (60% acrylic, 40% wool) bulky (chunky) yarn
  2 x 3½oz (100g) balls (120yd/110m) in shade 93 Methyl Blue

2 x 1-in (25-mm) white buttons or circles of white felt (see Safety note, opposite)

15 x 15in (38 x 38cm) pillow (cushion) pad

A few handfuls of 100% polyester toy filling

A very small amount of coral light worsted (DK) yarn

Black sewing thread

needles and equipment

US 10½ (7mm) knitting needles

Yarn sewing needle

Large-eyed embroidery needle

Standard sewing needle

gauge (tension)

12 sts and 14 rows in stockinette (stocking) stitch to a 4-in (10-cm) square on US 10½ (7mm) needles.

measurements

Cover will fit a 15 x 15in (38 x 38cm) pillow (cushion) pad.

abbreviations

See page 126.

to make pillow

First side

Cast on 45 sts.

Beg with a k row, work 50 rows in st st.

Row 51: Bind (cast) off 33 sts, k to end. *(12 sts)*

Beg with a p row, work 6 rows in st st.

Row 58: P6, WT.

Row 59: Knit.

Row 60: P7, WT.

Row 61: Knit.

Row 62: P8, WT.

Row 63: Knit.

Row 64: P9, WT.

Row 65: Knit.

Row 66: P10, WT.

Row 67: Knit.

Row 68: Purl.

*Row 69: K2, m1, k to last 2 sts, m1, k2 *(14 sts)*

Row 70: Purl.

Rep rows 69 70 once more. *(16 sts)*

Row 73: K2, m1, k6, turn and work on these 9 sts only, leaving rem 8 sts on needle.

Next row: Purl.

Next row: K2, m1, k to end. *(10 sts)*

Beg with a p row, work 5 rows in st st.

Next row: K2, k2tog, k2, ssk, k2. *(8 sts)*

Next row: P2tog, p4, p2tog. *(6 sts)*

Next row: K1, k2tog, ssk, k1. *(4 sts)*

Next row: [P2tog] twice. *(2 sts)*

Next row: K2tog. *(1 st)*

Fasten off.

Rejoin yarn to rem sts on RS of work.

Next row: K to last 2 sts, m1, k2. *(9 sts)*

Next row: Purl.

Rep last 2 rows once more. *(10 sts)*

Beg with a k row, work 4 rows in st st.

Next row: K2, k2tog, k2, ssk, k2. *(8 sts)*

Next row: P2tog, p4, p2tog. *(6 sts)*

Next row: K1, k2tog, ssk, k1. *(4 sts)*

Next row: [P2tog] twice. *(2 sts)*

Next row: K2tog. *(1 st)*

Fasten off.

Second side

Cast on 45 sts.

Beg with a k row, work 51 rows in st st.

Row 52: Bind (cast) off 33 sts pwise, p to end. *(12 sts)*

Beg with a k row, work 6 rows in st st.

Row 59: K6, WT.

Row 60: Purl.

Row 61: K7, WT.

Row 62: Purl.

Row 63: K8, WT.

Row 64: Purl.

Row 65: K9, WT.

Row 66: Purl

Row 67: K10, WT.

Row 68: Purl.

Work as for first side from * to end.

to make up

Place the two sides right sides together and oversew (see page 126) round the curved edges of the tail. Turn the cover right sides out and join the lower edges and sides using mattress stitch (see page 125), leaving the top open for inserting the pillow pad. Lightly stuff tail section. Insert the pad and close the top using mattress stitch.

Using coral yarn, embroider the mouth on both sides of the pillow using chain stitch (see page 124). Sew the buttons for the eyes firmly in place using black thread.

Safety note: buttons can be a choking hazard for small children. Sew the buttons securely and check them regularly, or if preferred, use circles of white felt instead of buttons, sewing them on with black thread.

Weave in all loose ends.

monkey
rattle

If you want a great alternative to shiny plastic or mainstream stroller toys, the obvious answer is to knit your own. I've knitted this monkey in one of my favorite baby-friendly yarns, which comes in a choice of colors to suit every taste. I've added a rattle inside to add a bit of interest—but that is strictly optional. If you want to customize your monkey, feel free to create your own colored stripes, or add a bit of texture to the handle.

yarn and materials
Cascade Cherub DK (55% nylon, 45% acrylic) light worsted (DK) yarn
  1 x 1¾oz (50g) ball (180yd/165m) in shade 17 Grey (A)
  1 x 1¾oz (50g) ball (180yd/165m) in shade 11 Key Lime (B)
  1 x 1¾oz (50g) ball (180yd/165m) in shade 14 Melon (C)

Very small amounts of black, white, and red light worsted (DK) yarns

A couple of handfuls of 100% polyester toy stuffing

A small toy rattle insert (available from toy-making suppliers or online)

needles and equipment
US 7 (4.5mm) knitting needles

US 3 (3.25) knitting needles

Yarn sewing needle

Large-eyed embroidery needle

gauge (tension)
18 sts and 22 rows in stockinette (stocking) stitch to a 4-in (10-cm) square on US 7 (4.5mm) needles when using yarn double.

measurements
The rattle is 7in (18cm) long.

abbreviations
See page 126.

to make pillow

Head

Make 2

Using US 7 (4.5mm) needles and yarn double, cast on 10 sts in A.

Row 1: [Inc] twice, k to last 3 sts, [inc] twice, k1. *(14 sts)*

Row 2: Purl.

Row 3: K2, m1, k1, m1, k to last 3 sts, m1, k1, m1, k2. *(18 sts)*

Row 4: Purl.

Row 5: K4, m1, k to last 4 sts, m1, k4. *(20 sts)*

Beg with a p row, work 13 rows in st st.

Row 19: K4, [k2tog] twice, k4, [ssk] twice, k4. *(16 sts)*

Row 20: [P2tog] twice, p8, [p2tog] twice. *(12 sts)*

Row 21: K2, [k2tog] twice, [ssk] twice, k2. *(8 sts)*

Bind (cast) off pwise.

Muzzle

Using US 7 (4.5mm) needles and yarn double, cast on 8 sts in A.

Row 1: K2, inc, k2, inc, k2. *(10 sts)*

Row 2: Purl.

Row 3: K2, m1, k to last 2 sts, m1, k2. *(12 sts)*

Row 4: Purl.

Row 5: K2, m1, k to last 2 sts, m1, k2. *(14 sts)*

Row 6: P2tog, p to last 2 sts, p2tog. *(12 sts)*

Row 7: K2, k2tog, k to last 4 sts, ssk, k2. *(10 sts)*

Row 8: P2tog, p to last 2 sts, p2tog. *(8 sts)*

Bind (cast) off.

Ear

Make 2

Using US 3 (3.25mm) needles, cast on 12 sts using a single strand of A.

Row 1: Purl.

Row 2: [K2tog] 3 times, [ssk] 3 times. *(6 sts)*

Row 3: [P2tog] 3 times. *(3 sts)*

Row 4: Sl1, k2tog, psso. *(1 st)*

Fasten off.

Handle

Using US 7 (4.5mm) needles and yarn double, cast on 18 sts in B.

Beg with a k row, work 6 rows in st st.

Leave B at side and join in yarn C, using it double.

Knit 2 rows.

Leave yarn C at the side and using B and beg with a k row, work 4 rows in st st.

Rep last 6 rows, 3 times more.

Beg with a k row, work 2 rows in st st in B.

Bind (cast) off.

to make up

Place the two head pieces right sides together and oversew (see page 126) round the sides and top, leaving the lower edge open. Turn the face the right way out and stuff. Tuck a little stuffing under the muzzle and oversew it and the ears in place using the photograph as a guide.

Join the long seam of the handle using mattress stitch (see page 125). Join the lower (cast-on) edge of the handle, again using mattress stitch. Stuff the handle.

Place the toy rattle insert inside the monkey's head. Oversew the lower edge of the head in place around the handle.

Using black yarn, work a small coil of chain stitch (see page 124) for the centers of the eyes. Using white yarn, work a circle of chain stitch around the eye centers. Using red yarn, work a line of chain stitch for the mouth.

Weave in all loose ends.

aardvark

This little knitted African mammal would make a great companion for anyone who finds teddies and bunnies… well, just a little too cute. I've chosen a deep mauve wool-mix yarn for this one, but you could knit him (or her) in any color you want. Aardvarks are a great way of using up oddments in your stash, so why not knit yourself a whole family?

yarn and materials

Sirdar Country Style DK (40% nylon, 30% wool, 30% acrylic) light worsted (DK) yarn 1 x 1¾oz (50g) ball (170yd/155m) in shade 615 Purple Sage

Very small amounts of black and white light worsted (DK) yarn

A few handfuls of 100% polyester toy filling

needles and equipment

US 3 (3.25mm) knitting needles

2 x stitch markers or small safety pins

Yarn sewing needle

Large-eyed embroidery needle

gauge (tension)

24 sts and 32 rows in stockinette (stocking) stitch to a 4-in (10-cm) square on US 3 (3.25mm) needles.

measurements

The finished toy is 8in (20cm) long (excluding tail).

abbreviations

See page 126.

to make aardvark

First side

Cast on 6 sts for front leg.
Beg with a k row, work 8 rows in st st.
Row 9: K1, m1, k to last st, m1, k1. (8 sts)
Row 10: Purl.
Rep rows 9–10 once more. (10 sts)
Break yarn and leave sts on needle.
On needle with sts, cast on another 6 sts for back leg.
Beg with a k row, work 6 rows in st st.
Row 7: K to last st, m1, k1. (7 sts)
Row 8: Purl.
Rep rows 7–8 once more. (8 sts)
Next row: K8 sts from back leg, turn work and cast on 16 sts, turn work back and k9 from front leg, m1, k1. (35 sts)
Next row: Purl.
Next row: K to last 2 sts, m1, k1, m1, k1. (37 sts)
Next row: Purl.*
Rep last 2 rows twice more. (41 sts)
Next row: K to last 2 sts, m1, k1, m1, k1. (43 sts)
Next row: Cast on 12 sts at beg of row, p to end. (55 sts)

Beg with a k row, work 5 rows in st st.
Next row: Bind (cast) off 4 sts pwise, p to end. (51 sts)
Next row: K2, k2tog, k to end. (50 sts)
Next row: Bind (cast) off 4 sts pwise, p to end. (46 sts)
Next row: Knit.
Next row: Bind (cast) off 4 sts pwise, p to end. (42 sts)
Next row: K2, k2tog, k to end. (41 sts)
Next row: Bind (cast) off 4 sts pwise, p to end. (37 sts)
Next row: K2, k2tog, k to end. (36 sts)
Next row: Bind (cast) off 4 sts pwise, p to end. (32 sts)
Next row: Bind (cast) off 4 sts, k to end. (28 sts)
Next row: Bind (cast) off 4 sts pwise, p to end. (24 sts)
Bind (cast) off.

Second side

Cast on 6 sts for back leg.
Beg with a k row, work 6 rows in st st.
Row 7: K1, m1, k to end. (7 sts)
Row 8: Purl.
Rep rows 7–8 once more. (8 sts)
Break yarn and leave sts on needle.

On needle with sts, cast on another 6 sts for front leg.

Beg with a k row, work 8 rows in st st.

Row 9: K1, m1, k to last st, m1, k1. (8 sts)

Row 10: Purl.

Rep last 2 rows once more. (10 sts)

Next row: K1, m1, k rem 9 sts from front leg, turn work and cast on 16 sts, turn work back and k8 from back leg. (35 sts)

Next row: Purl.

Next row: [K1, m1] twice, k to end. (37 sts)

Next row: Purl.

Rep last 2 rows twice more. (41 sts)

Next row: [K1, m1] twice, k to end. (43 sts)

Next row: Purl.

Next row: Cast on 12 sts at beg of row, k to end. (55 sts)

Beg with a p row, work 5 rows in st st.

Next row: Bind (cast) off 4 sts, k to last 4 sts, ssk, k2. (50 sts)

Next row: Purl.

Next row: Bind (cast) off 4 sts, k to end. (46 sts)

Next row: Purl.

Next row: Bind (cast) off 4 sts, k to last 4 sts, ssk, k2. (41 sts)

Next row: Purl.

Next row: Bind (cast) off 4 sts, k to last 4 sts, ssk, k2. (36 sts)

Next row: Bind (cast) off 4 sts pwise, p to end. (32 sts)

Next row: Bind (cast) off 4 sts, k to end. (28 sts)

Next row: Bind (cast) off 4 sts pwise, p to end. (24 sts)

Bind (cast) off.

Gusset

Work as for first side to *.

Next row: K to last 2 sts, m1, k1, m1, k1. (39 sts)

Next row: Purl.

Next row: K to last 5 sts, [k2tog] twice, k1. (37 sts)

Next row: Purl.

Rep last 2 rows once more. (35 sts)

Next row: K8, turn, work on these 8 sts only, leaving rem sts on needle.

Next row: P2tog, p to end. (7 sts)

Next row: Knit.

Next row: P2tog, p to end. (6 sts)

Beg with a k row, work 6 rows in st st.

Bind (cast) off.

Rejoin yarn to rem 27 sts on RS of work.

Next row: Bind (cast) off 16 sts, k to last 3 sts, k2tog, k1. (10 sts)

Next row: P2tog, p to last 2 sts, p2tog. (8 sts)

Next row: Knit.

Next row: P2tog, p to last 2 sts, p2tog. (6 sts)

Beg with a k row, work 8 rows in st st.

Bind (cast) off.

Tail

Cast on 12 sts.

Beg with a k row, work 8 rows in st st.

Row 9: K1, k2tog, k to last 3 sts, ssk, k1. (10 sts)

Beg with a p row, work 5 rows in st st.

Rep rows 9–14 (last 6 rows) once more. (8 sts)

Row 21: K1, k2tog, k to last 2 sts, ssk, k1. (6 sts)

Beg with a p row, work 3 rows in st st.

Row 25: K1, k2tog, ssk, k1. (4 sts)

Row 26: [P2tog] twice. (2 sts)

Row 27: K2tog. (1 st)

Fasten off.

Ear

Make 4

Cast on 5 sts.

Beg with a k row, work 8 rows in st st.

Row 9: Ssk, k1, k2tog. (3 sts)

Row 10: P3tog. (1 st)

Fasten off.

to make up

Fold the gusset piece in half lengthwise and mark each end of the fold with a stitch marker or small safety pin. This will mark the center line of the gusset—one half will be sewn to one side of the lower part of the body; the other half will be sewn to the second side of the body. Pin the gusset in position, so the right sides of your work are together. Oversew (see page 126) or backstitch in place.

Oversew or backstitch the remaining parts of the body together, leaving a gap in the top for turning and stuffing. Turn and stuff. Stitch the gap closed.

Sew the long seam of the tail using mattress stitch (see page 125). Stuff lightly and oversew in position.

Place two ear pieces right sides together and oversew around the curved edges, leaving lower edges open. Repeat for the second ear. Turn the ears the right way out and sew in position, using the photograph as a guide.

Using black yarn, work two French knots (see page 124) for the eye centers. Using a separated strand of white yarn, work a few coils of chain stitch (see page 124) around each eye center.

Weave in all loose ends.

turtle rug

If you're looking for a nifty rug to complement an ocean-themed bedroom or nursery, this turtle rug is just the ticket. It's cute, but not too cute— so suitable for self-respecting toddlers as well as younger babies. The shell is knitted in a type of cable stitch, but don't be put off by that because as the yarn is super-bulky, it's easy to see what's going on.

yarn and materials

Lion Brand Hometown USA (100% acrylic) super-bulky (super-chunky) yarn
  2 x 5oz (142g) balls (80yd/74m) in shade 172 Oklahoma City Green (A)
  1 5oz (142g) ball (80yd/74m) in shade 170 Las Vegas Gold (B)

Small amounts of black, white, and red light worsted (DK) yarns

½yd (0.5m) of 59-in (150-cm) wide polyester fleece fabric in beige

Beige sewing thread

needles and equipment

US 11 (8mm) knitting needles

US L-11 (8mm) crochet hook

Cable needle

Yarn sewing needle

Large-eyed embroidery needle

Water-soluble pen or quilters' pencil

Some pins

gauge (tension)

10 sts and 13 rows in stockinette (stocking) stitch to a 4-in (10-cm) square on US 11 (8mm) needles.

measurements

The rug is 29in (74cm) long from nose to tail.

abbreviations

C4B = cable four back. Slip next 2 sts onto cable needle and hold at back of work, knit next 2 sts from LH needle, knit 2 sts from cable needle.

C4F = cable four front. Slip next 2 sts onto cable needle and hold at front of work, knit next 2 sts from LH needle, knit 2 sts from cable needle.

See also page 126.

to make rug

Shell

Cast on 14 sts in A.

Row 1: Inc, k to last 2 sts, inc, k1. *(16 sts)*
Row 2 and every WS row unless otherwise stated: Purl
Row 3: K1, m1, k to last st, m1, k1. *(18 sts)*
Row 5: K1, m1, [C4B, C4F] twice, m1, k1. *(20 sts)*
Row 7: K1, m1, k to last st, m1, k1. *(22 sts)*
Row 9: K1, m1, k2, [C4F, C4B] twice, k2, m1, k1. *(24 sts)*

Row 11: K1, m1, k to last st, m1, k1. *(26 sts)*
Row 13: K1, m1, C4F, [C4B, C4F] twice, C4B, m1, k1. *(28 sts)*
Row 15: K1, m1, k to last st, m1, k1. *(30 sts)*
Row 17: K1, m1, k2, C4B, [C4F, C4B] twice, C4F, k2, m1, k1. *(32 sts)*
Row 19: K1, m1, k to last st, m1, k1. *(34 sts)*
Row 21: K1, m1, [C4B, C4F] 4 times, m1, k1. *(36 sts)*
Row 23: K1, m1, k to last st, m1, k1. *(38 sts)*
Row 25: K1, m1, k2, [C4F, C4B] 4 times, k2, m1, k1. *(40 sts)*
Row 27: K1, m1, k to last st, m1, k1. *(42 sts)*

Row 29: K1, m1, C4F, [C4B, C4F] 4 times, C4B, m1, k1. *(44 sts)*
Row 31: K1, m1, k to last st, m1, k1. *(46 sts)*
Row 33: K1, m1, k2, C4B, [C4F, C4B] 4 times, C4F, k2, m1, k1. *(48 sts)*
Row 35: K1, m1, k to last st, m1, k1. *(50 sts)*
Row 37: K1, m1, [C4B, C4F] 6 times, m1, k1. *(52 sts)*
Beg with a p row, work 3 rows in st st.
Row 41: K2, [C4F, C4B] 6 times, k2.
Beg with a p row, work 3 rows in st st.
Row 45: K2, [C4B, C4F] 6 times, k2.
Beg with a p row, work 3 rows in st st.
Rep rows 41–44 once more.
Row 53: K2tog, [C4B, C4F] 6 times, ssk. *(50 sts)*
Row 54: P2tog, p to last 2 sts, p2tog. *(48 sts)*
Row 55: K2tog, k to last 2 sts, ssk. *(46 sts)*
Row 56: P2tog, p to last 2 sts, p2tog. *(44 sts)*
Row 57: K2tog, C4B, [C4F, C4B] 4 times, C4F, ssk. *(42 sts)*
Rep rows 54–56 once more. *(36 sts)*
Row 61: K2tog, C4B, [C4F, C4B] 3 times, C4F, ssk. *(34 sts)*
Rep rows 54–56 once more. *(28 sts)*
Row 65: K2tog, C4B, [C4F, C4B] twice, C4F, ssk. *(26 sts)*
Row 66: P2 tog, p to last 2 sts, p2tog. *(24 sts)*
Row 67: K2tog, k to last 2 sts, ssk. *(22 sts)*
Row 68: [P2tog] twice, p to last 4 sts, [p2tog] twice. *(18 sts)*
Bind (cast) off.

Head

Cast on 12 sts in B.
Beg with a k row, work 6 rows in st st.
Row 7: K1, k2tog, k6, ssk, k1. *(10 sts)*
Row 8: Purl.
Row 9: K1, k2tog, k4, ssk, k1. *(8 sts)*
Row 10: P2tog, p4, p2tog. *(6 sts)*
Row 11: K1, k2tog, ssk, k1. *(4 sts)*
Bind (cast) off pwise.

First front leg

Cast on 12 sts in B.
Row 1: Inc, k to end. *(13 sts)*
Row 2: Purl.
Row 3: K2, m1, k to end. *(14 sts)*
Row 4: Purl.
Rep rows 3–4, 3 times more. *(17 sts)*
Row 11: K2, m1, k to end. *(18 sts)*
Row 12: Bind (cast) off 9 sts pwise, p to end. *(9 sts)*
Row 13: K2, m1, k to last 2 sts, ssk, k2.
Row 14: Purl.
Rep rows 13–14 twice more.
*****Row 19:** K1, k2tog, k3, ssk, k1. *(7 sts)*
Row 20: Purl.

Row 21: K1, k2tog, k1, ssk, k1. *(5 sts)*
Row 22: Purl.
Row 25: K2tog, k1, ssk. *(3 sts)*
Row 26: Purl.
Row 27: Sl1, k2tog, psso. *(1 st)*
Fasten off.

Second front leg

Cast on 12 sts in B.
Row 1: K to last 2 sts, inc, k1. *(13 sts)*
Row 2: Purl.
Row 3: K to last 2 sts, m1, k2. *(14 sts)*
Row 4: Purl.
Rep rows 3–4, 4 times. *(18 sts)*
Row 13: Bind (cast) off 10 sts, k to last 2 sts, m1, k2. *(9 sts)*
Row 14: Purl.
Row 15: K2, k2tog, k to last 2 sts, m1, k2.
Row 16: Purl.
Rep rows 15–16 once more.
Work as for first front leg from * to end.

Back leg

The back legs are knitted from the top (the part near the shell) downward.
Make 2
Cast on 3 sts in B.
Row 1: [Inc] twice, k1. *(5 sts)*
Row 2: Purl.
Row 3: K1, m1, k3, m1, k1. *(7 sts)*
Beg with a p row, work 11 rows in st st.
Row 15: K1, k2tog, k1, ssk, k1. *(5 sts)*
Row 16: P2tog, p1, p2tog. *(3 sts)*
Row 17: K3tog tbl. *(1 st)*
Fasten off.

Tail

Cast on 7 sts in B.
Row 1: Purl.
Row 2: K2tog, k3, ssk. *(5 sts)*
Row 3: Purl.
Row 4: K2tog, k1, ssk. *(3 sts)*
Row 5: Purl.
Row 6: K3tog. *(1 st)*
Fasten off.

to make up

Using matching yarn, use the crochet hook to work a crochet edge (see page 122) around the entire shell, around the sides and top of the head (leaving the lower edge where it will be attached to the shell unworked), and the sides of the front legs (leaving the lower edge where they will be attached to the shell unworked). Then work a crochet edge around the back legs, leaving the right-hand side of the top of one leg unworked and the left-hand side of the top of the other leg unworked. The edges left unworked will be attached to the shell.

Weave in all loose ends.

Lay shell on beige fleece and draw around the shape with the water-soluble pen or quilters' pencil. Cut shape out. Pin the fleece fabric in place on the underside of the rug, with the right side of the fabric facing outward. Tuck the raw edges of the fleece under and slip stitch in place around the outer edges of the rug, just inside the crochet edge.

Stitch the head, legs, and tail in place, using the photograph as a guide. Using black yarn, work two small coils of chain stitch (see page 124) for the eye centers. Using white yarn, work a circle of chain stitch around the eye center. Using red yarn, work a curved line of chain stitch for the mouth.

techniques

On the following pages you'll find the basic knitting techniques that you will need for most of the patterns in this book. The knitting needles, yarn, and other items that you need to make each project are listed at the beginning of the relevant pattern instructions. You can substitute the yarn recommended in a pattern with the same weight of yarn in a different brand, but you will need to check the gauge (tension) (see below). When calculating the quantity of yarn you require, it is the length of yarn in each ball that you need to check, rather than the weight of the ball; the length of yarn in each ball of the recommended project yarn is given in the materials list for the pattern.

If you are substituting brands for a very small amount of yarn—for example, to embroider a nose or eyes—this will hardly affect the look of your project at all, and it is very sensible to use up yarns you have in your stash.

Baby and toddler sizing guide

The age range for the patterns is a guide only and they have been designed according to the following guide. If in doubt, knit an item in the larger size if possible. If you fall in love with a pattern but it is not available in the size you need, please get in touch via Fiona's website, fionagoble.com, as she may be able to help.

Baby clothes

Age	Height	Weight
3–6 months	up to 27in (68cm)	18lb (8kg)
6–9 months	up to 29in (74cm)	20lb (9kg)
9–12 months	up to 31½in (80cm)	25lb (11kg)
12–18 months	up to 34in (86cm)	26½lb (12kg)

Toddler clothes

Age	Chest measurement
12–18 months	up to 20½in (52cm)
2–3 years	up to 21½in (54cm)

Gauge (tension)

A gauge (tension) is given with each pattern to help you make your item the same size as the sample. The gauge (tension) is given as the number of stitches and rows you need to work to produce a 4-in (10-cm) square of knitting.

Using the recommended yarn and needles, cast on 8 stitches more than the gauge (tension) instruction asks for—so if you need to have 10 stitches to 4in (10cm), cast on 18 stitches. Working in pattern as instructed, work eight rows more than is needed. Bind (cast) off loosely.

Lay the swatch flat without stretching it. Lay a ruler across the stitches as shown, with the 2in (5cm) mark centered on the knitting, then put a pin in the knitting at the start of the ruler and at the 4in (10cm) mark: the pins should be well away from the edges of the swatch. Count the number of stitches between the pins. Repeat the process across the rows to count the number of rows to 4in (10cm).

If the number of stitches and rows you've counted is the same as the number asked for in the instructions, you have

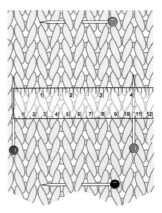

the correct gauge (tension). If you do not have the same number then you will need to change your gauge (tension).

To change gauge (tension) you need to change the size of your knitting needles. A good rule of thumb to follow is that one difference in needle size will create a difference of one stitch in the gauge (tension). You will need to use larger needles to achieve fewer stitches and smaller ones to achieve more stitches.

Holding needles

If you are a knitting novice, you will need to discover which is the most comfortable way for you to hold your needles.

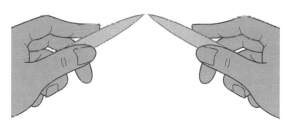

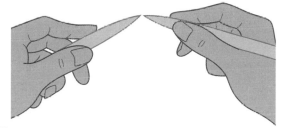

Like a knife

Pick up the needles, one in each hand, as if you were holding a knife and fork—that is to say, with your hands lightly over the top of each needle. As you knit, you will tuck the blunt end of the right-hand needle under your arm, let go with your hand, and use your hand to manipulate the yarn, returning your hand to the needle to move the stitches along.

Like a pen

Now try changing the right hand so you are holding the needle as you would hold a pen, with your thumb and forefinger lightly gripping the needle close to its pointed tip and the shaft resting in the crook of your thumb. As you knit, you will not need to let go of the needle but simply slide your right hand forward to manipulate the yarn.

Holding yarn

As you knit, you will be working stitches off the left-hand needle and onto the right-hand needle, and the yarn you are working with needs to be tensioned and manipulated to produce an even fabric. To hold and tension the yarn you can use either your right or left hand, depending on the method you are going to use to make the stitches.

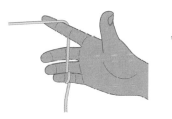

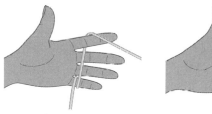

Yarn in right hand

To knit and purl in the US/UK style (see pages 117 and 118), hold the yarn in your right hand. You can wind the yarn around your fingers in different ways, depending on how tightly you need to hold it to achieve an even gauge (tension). Try both ways shown to find out which works best for you.

To hold the yarn tightly (left), wind it right around your little finger, under your ring and middle fingers, then pass it over your index finger, which will manipulate the yarn.

For a looser hold (right), catch the yarn between your little and ring fingers, pass it under your middle finger, then over your index finger.

Yarn in left hand

To knit and purl in the continental style (see pages 117 and 118), hold the yarn in your left hand. This method is sometimes easier for left-handed people to use, though many left-handers are quite comfortable knitting with the yarn in their right hand. Try the ways shown to find out which works best for you.

To hold the yarn tightly (left), wind it right around your little finger, under your ring and middle fingers, then pass it over your index finger, which will manipulate the yarn.

For a looser hold (right), fold your little, ring, and middle fingers over the yarn, and wind it twice around your index finger.

Making a slip knot

You will need to make a slip knot to form your first cast-on stitch.

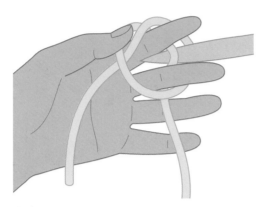

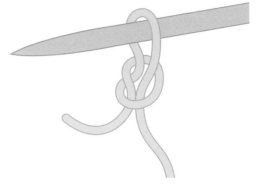

1 With the ball of yarn on your right, lay the end of the yarn on the palm of your left hand and hold it in place with your left thumb. With your right hand, take the yarn around your top two fingers to form a loop. Take the knitting needle through the back of the loop from right to left and use it to pick up the strand nearest to the yarn ball, as shown in the diagram. Pull the strand through to form a loop at the front.

2 Slip the yarn off your fingers, leaving the loop on the needle. Gently pull on both yarn ends to tighten the knot. Then pull on the yarn leading to the ball of yarn to tighten the knot on the needle.

Casting on (cable method)

There are a few methods of casting on but the one used for the projects in this book is the cable method, which uses two needles.

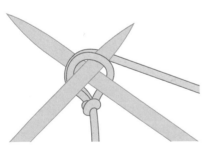

1 Make a slip knot as shown above. Put the needle with the slip knot into your left hand. Insert the point of the other needle into the front of the slip knot and under the left-hand needle. Wind the yarn from the ball of yarn around the tip of the right-hand needle.

2 Using the tip of the needle, draw the yarn through the slip knot to form a loop. This loop is the new stitch. Slip the loop from the right-hand needle onto the left-hand needle.

3 To make the next stitch, insert the tip of the right-hand needle between the two stitches. Wind the yarn over the right-hand needle, from left to right, then draw the yarn through to form a loop. Transfer this loop to the left-hand needle. Repeat until you have cast on the right number of stitches for the project.

Knit stitch

There are only two stitches to master in knitting; knit stitch and purl stitch. Most people in the English-speaking world knit using a method called English (or American) knitting. However, in parts of Europe, people prefer a method known as Continental knitting.

US/UK style

1 Hold the needle with the cast-on stitches in your left hand, and then insert the point of the right-hand needle into the front of the first stitch from left to right. Wind the yarn around the point of the right hand needle, from left to right.

2 With the tip of the right-hand needle, pull the yarn through the stitch to form a loop. This loop is the new stitch

3 Slip the original stitch off the left-hand needle by gently pulling the right-hand needle to the right. Repeat these steps till you have knitted all the stitches on the left hand needle. To work the next row, transfer the needle with all the stitches into your left hand.

Continental style

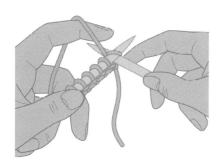 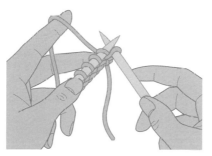 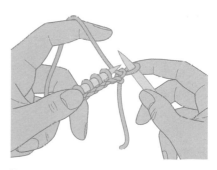

1 Hold the needle with the stitches to be knitted in your left hand, and then insert the tip of the right-hand needle into the front of the first stitch from left to right. Holding the yarn fairly taut with your left hand at the back of your work, use the tip of the right-hand needle to pick up a loop of yarn.

2 With the tip of the right-hand needle, bring the yarn through the original stitch to form a loop. This loop is the new stitch.

3 Slip the original stitch off the left-hand needle by gently pulling the right-hand needle to the right. Repeat these steps till you have knitted all the stitches on the left-hand needle. To work the next row, transfer the needle with all the stitches into your left hand.

Purl stitch

As with knit stitch, purl stitch can be formed in two ways. If you are new to knitting, try both techniques to see which works better for you: left-handed people may find the Continental method easier to master.

US/UK style

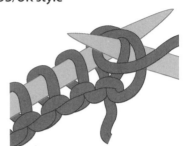  

1 Hold the needle with the stitches in your left hand, and then insert the point of the right-hand needle into the front of the first stitch from right to left. Wind the yarn around the point of the right-hand needle, from right to left.

2 With the tip of the right-hand needle, pull the yarn through the stitch to form a loop. This loop is the new stitch.

3 Slip the original stitch off the left-hand needle by gently pulling the right-hand needle to the right. Repeat these steps till you have purled all the stitches on the left-hand needle. To work the next row, transfer the needle with all the stitches into your left hand.

Continental style

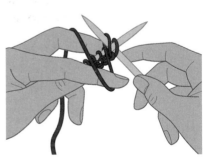  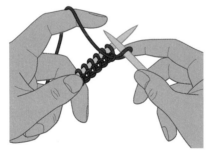

1 Hold the needle with the stitches to be knitted in your left hand, and then insert the tip of the right-hand needle into the front of the first stitch from right to left. Holding the yarn fairly taut at the front of the work, move the tip of the right-hand needle under the working yarn, then push your left index finger downward, as shown, to hold the yarn around the needle.

2 With the tip of the right-hand needle, bring the yarn through the original stitch to form a loop.

3 Slip the original stitch off the left-hand needle by gently pulling the right-hand needle to the right. Repeat these steps till you have purled all the stitches on the left-hand needle. To work the next row, transfer the needle with all the stitches into your left hand.

Binding (casting) off

You need to bind (cast) off the stitches to complete the projects and stop the knitting unraveling.

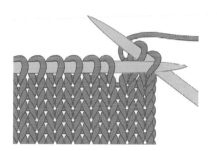

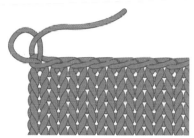

1 First knit two stitches in the normal way. With the point of the left hand needle, pick up the first stitch you have just knitted and lift it over the second stitch. Knit another stitch so that there are two stitches on the right-hand needle

again. Repeat the process of lifting the first stitch over the second stitch. Continue this process until there is just one stitch remaining on the right-hand needle.

2 Break the yarn, leaving a tail of yarn long enough to sew the work together (see page 125). Pull the tail all the way through the last stitch. Slip the stitch off the needle and pull it fairly tightly to make sure it is secure.

Slipping stitches

This means moving stitches from one needle to the other without knitting or purling them. They can be slipped knitwise or purlwise depending on the row you are working, or any specific pattern instructions.

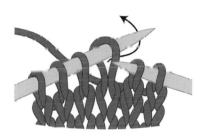

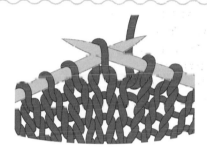

Knitwise

From left to right, put the right-hand needle into the next stitch on the left-hand needle (as shown by the arrow) and slip it across onto the right-hand needle without working it.

Purlwise

You can slip a stitch purlwise on a purl row or a knit row. From right to left, put the right-hand needle into the next stitch on the left-hand needle and slip it across onto the right-hand needle without working it.

Picking up stitches

For some projects, you will need to pick up stitches along either a horizontal edge (the cast-on or bound-/cast-off edge of your knitting), or a vertical edge (the edges of your rows of knitting).

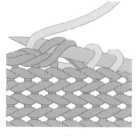

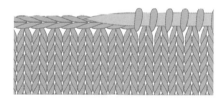

Along a row-end edge

With the right side of the knitting facing you, insert a knitting needle from the front to back between the first and second stitches of the first row. Wind the yarn around the needle and pull through a loop to form the new stitch. Normally you have more gaps between rows than stitches you need to pick up and knit. To make sure your picking up is even, you will have to miss a gap every few rows.

Along a cast-on or bound- (cast-) off edge

This is worked in the same way as picking up stitches along a vertical edge, except that you will work through the cast-on stitches rather than the gaps between rows. You will normally have the same number of stitches to pick up and knit as there are existing stitches.

Yarnover (yo)

To make a yarnover you wind the yarn around the right-hand needle to make an extra loop that is worked as a stitch on the next row.

Bring the yarn between the tips of the needles to the front. Take the yarn over the right-hand needle to the back and knit the next stitch on the left-hand needle (see page 117).

Increasing

There are three methods of increasing used in projects in this book.

Increase on a knit row (inc)

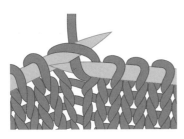

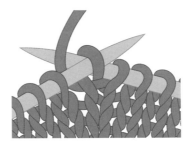

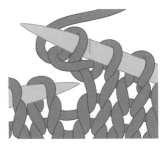

1 Knit the next stitch on the left-hand needle in the usual way (see page 117), but do not slip the "old" stitch off the left-hand needle.

2 Move the right-hand needle behind the left-hand needle and put it into the same stitch again, but through the back of the stitch this time. Knit the stitch again.

3 Now slip the "old" stitch off the left-hand needle in the usual way.

Increase on a purl row (inc pwise)

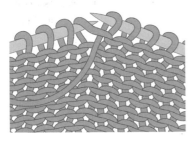

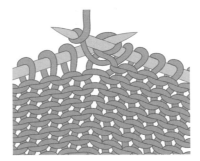

1 Purl the next stitch on the left-hand needle in the usual way (see page 118), but do not slip the "old" stitch off the left-hand needle.

2 Twist the right-hand needle backward to make it easier to put it into the same stitch again, but through the back of the stitch this time. Purl the stitch again, then slip the "old" stitch off the left-hand needle in the usual way.

Make one stitch (m1)

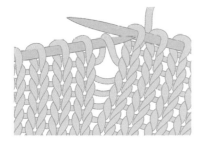 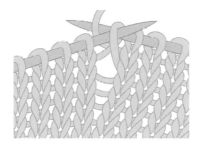

1 From the front, slip the tip of the left-hand needle under the horizontal strand of yarn running between the last stitch on the right-hand needle and the first stitch on the left-hand needle.

2 Put the right-hand needle knitwise into the back of the loop formed by the picked-up strand and knit into it in the normal way. (It is important to knit into the back of the loop so that it is twisted and a hole does not form in your work.)

Decreasing

There are five different ways of decreasing used in this book, one of which decreases by two stitches rather than one stitch.

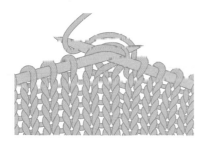 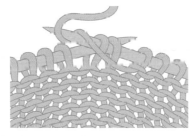

Knit two together (k2tog)

This is the simplest way of decreasing. Simply insert the right-hand needle through two stitches instead of the normal one, and then knit them in the usual way.

The same principle is used to knit three stitches together; just insert the right-hand needle through three instead of through two.

Purl two together (p2tog)

To make a simple decrease on a purl row, insert the right-hand needle through two stitches instead of the normal one, and then purl them in the usual way.

Knit or purl three together (k/p3tog)

This is done in the same way as knitting or purling two stitches together, but insert the right-hand needle through three stitches instead of two.

Purl two together through the back loops (p2tog tbl)

This is done in the same way as p2tog, but insert the right-hand needle through the back loops of both the purl stitches. This can be a bit tricky as the stitches will be tight, so put the needle through them in the usual way first and gently stretch them a little.

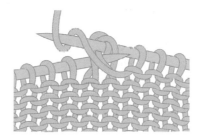

Slip, slip, knit (ssk)

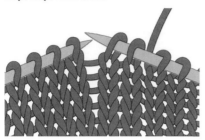

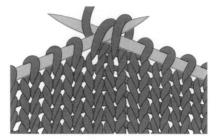

1 Slip one stitch knitwise, and then the next stitch knitwise onto the right-hand needle, without knitting them.

2 Insert the left-hand needle from left to right through the front loops of both the slipped stitches and knit them in the usual way.

Crochet techniques

While the projects in this book are all knitted rather than crocheted, a few of them require simple crochet chains or edging.

Crochet chain

1 Make a slip knot on the crochet hook in the same way as for knitting (see page 116). Holding the slip knot on the hook, wind the yarn around the hook from the back to the front, then catch the yarn in the crochet-hook tip.

2 Pull the yarn through the slip knot on the crochet hook to make the second link in the chain. Continue in this way till the chain is the length needed.

Crochet edging

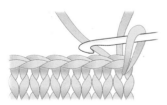

1 A crochet edging can be worked along a horizontal edge or a vertical edge, but the basic technique is the same. Insert the crochet hook in the first space between stitches. Wind the yarn round the hook and pull a loop of yarn through.

2 Wind the yarn round the hook again and then pull the loop through to make a single chain.

3 Insert the hook through the next stitch, wind the yarn round the hook, and pull through a second loop of yarn.

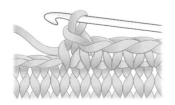

4 Wind the yarn round the hook and pull a loop of yarn through both loops on the hook. Repeat steps 3 and 4, inserting the hook into the spaces between stitches in an even pattern.

For crochet edging along a vertical edge, insert your hook into the spaces between the edges of the rows rather than the spaces between stitches.

Knitting in different colors

It's important to change colors in the right way to keep the knitted fabric flat and smooth and without any holes.

Intarsia

If you are knitting blocks of different colors within a project then you will need to use a technique called intarsia. This involves having separate balls of yarn for each area and twisting the yarns together where they join to avoid creating a hole or gap.

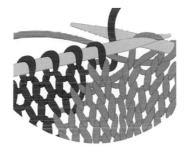

On the right side
When you want to change colors in a vertical line or sloping to the right, take the first color over the second color. Then pick up the second color, so the strands of yarn cross each other.

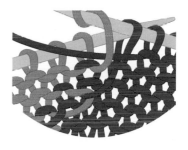

On the wrong side
On this side it is easy to see how the yarns are linked at each color change.

When you want to change colors and the color change is vertical or sloping to the left, take the first color over the second color. Then pick up the second color, so the strands of yarn cross each other.

Stranding

If you are knitting just a few stitches in a different color, you can simply leave the color you are not using on the wrong side of the work and pick it up again when you need to.

Changing color on a knit row

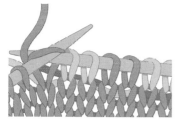

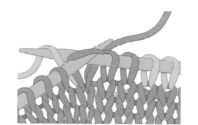

1 Knit the stitches (see page 117) in color A (brown in this example), bringing the yarn across over the strand of color B (lime) to wrap around the needle.

2 At the color change, drop color A and pick up color B, bringing it across under the strand of color A to wrap around the needle. Be careful not to pull it too tight. Knit the stitches in color B. When you change back to color A, bring it across over the strand of color B.

Changing color on a purl row

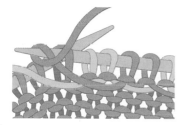

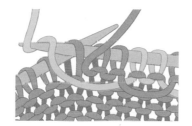

1 Purl the stitches (see page 118) in color A (brown), bringing it across over color B (lime) to wrap around the needle.

2 At the color change, drop color A and pick up color B, bringing it across under the strand of color A to wrap around the needle. Be careful not to pull it too tight. Purl the stitches in color B. When you change back to color A, bring it across over the strand of color B.

I-cord

This type of cord is knitted on two double-pointed needles. The number of stitches can vary depending on how thick you want the i-cord to be, and a firm gauge (tension) works best.

1 Cast on as many stitches as needed; here there are four. *Slide the stitches to the right-hand end of the double-pointed needle, with the working yarn on the left of the cast-on row. Pull the yarn tightly across the back of the stitches and knit the first stitch as firmly as you can, then knit the remaining stitches.

2 Repeat from * until the i-cord is the length you need. After the first couple of rows, it will be easy to pull the yarn neatly across the back of the stitches for an invisible join in the cord.

Embroidery stitches

The animals' features are embroidered using knitting yarn. When embroidering on knitting, take the embroidery needle in and out of the work between the strands that make up the yarn rather than between the knitted stitches themselves; this will help make your embroidery look more even.

Chain stitch

Bring the yarn out at the starting point on the front of the work. Take your needle back into your knitting just next to the starting point, leaving a loop of yarn. Bring your needle out of the work again, a stitch length farther on and catch in the loop. Pull the thread up firmly, but not so tight that it pulls the knitting. Continue in this way till the line, coil, or circle is complete.

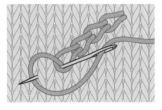

Straight stitch

To make this stitch, simply take the yarn out at the starting point and back down into the work where you want the stitch to end.

French knot

1 Bring the yarn out at the starting point, where you want the French knot to sit. Wind the yarn around your needle the required number of times.

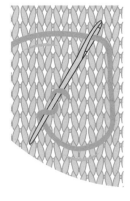

2 Take the needle back into the work, just to the side of the starting point. Then bring your needle out at the point for the next French knot or, if you are working the last or a single knot, to the back of your work. Continue pulling your needle through the work and slide the knot off the needle and onto the knitting.

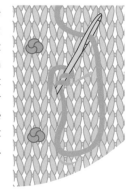

Sewing seams

There are various sewing-up stitches, and the patterns advise you on which method to use.

Mattress stitch on row-end edges

1 Right-sides up, lay the edges to be joined side by side. Thread a yarn sewing needle and from the back, bring it up between the first and second stitches of the left-hand piece, immediately above the cast-on edge. Take it across to the right-hand piece, and from the back bring it through between the first two stitches, immediately above the cast-on

edge. Take it back to the left-hand piece and from the back, bring it through where it first came out. Pull the yarn through and this figure-eight will hold the cast-on edges level. Take the needle across to the right-hand piece and, from the front, take it under the bars of yarn between the first and second stitches on the next two rows up.

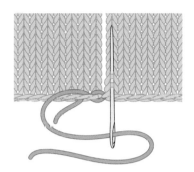

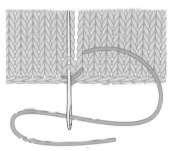

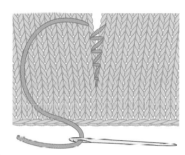

2 Take the needle across to the left-hand piece and, from the front, take it under the bars of yarn between the first and second stitches on the next two rows up. Continue in this way, taking the needle under two bars on one piece and then the other, to sew up the seam.

3 When you have sewn about 1in (2.5cm), gently and evenly pull the stitches tight to close the seam, and then continue to complete the sewing.

Mattress stitch on cast-on and bound- (cast-) off edges

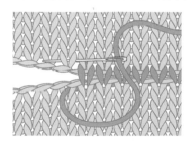

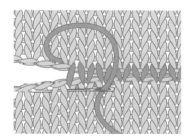

1 Right-sides up, lay the two edges to be joined side by side. Thread a yarn sewing needle with a tail left after binding (casting) off, or a long length of yarn.

Secure the yarn on the back of the lower knitted piece, then bring the needle up through the middle of the first whole stitch in that piece. Take the needle under both "legs" of the first whole stitch on the upper piece, so that it comes to the front between the first and second stitches.

2 Go back into the lower piece and take the needle through to the back where it first came out, and then bring it back to the front in the middle of the next stitch along. Pull the yarn through. Take the needle under both "legs" of the next whole stitch on the upper piece. Repeat this step to sew the seam. Pull the stitches gently taut to close the seam as you work.

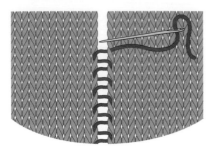

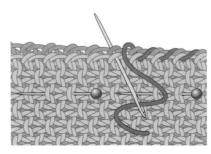

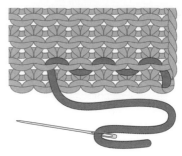

Flat stitch

This stitch creates a join that is completely flat.

Right-sides up, lay the two edges to be joined side by side. Thread a yarn sewing needle with a tail left after binding (casting) off, or a long length of yarn. Pick up the very outermost strand of knitting from one piece and then the same strand on the other piece. Work your way along the seam, pulling the yarn up firmly every few stitches to close the seam.

Oversewing

This stitch can be worked with the right or the wrong sides of the work together. Thread a yarn sewing needle with a tail left after binding (casting) off, or a long length of yarn. Bring the yarn from the back of the work, over the edge of the knitting, and out through to the back again a short distance farther on.

Sewing in ends

The easiest way to finish yarn ends is to run a few small stitches forward then backward through your work, ideally in a seam. It is a good idea to use a yarn sewing needle to do this and take the tail between the strands that make up your yarn, as this will help make sure the end stays in place.

abbreviations

approx.	approximately
beg	begin(ning)
C4B	cable four back
C4F	cable four forward
cm	centimeter(s)
cont	continue
foll(s)	follow(s)(ing)
g	gram(s)
in	inch(es)
inc	increase on a knit row: see page 120
inc pwise	increase on a purl row: see page 120
k	knit
k2tog	knit two stitches together: see page 121
k3tog	knit three stitches together: see page 121
kwise	knitwise
LH	left-hand
m	meter(s)
m1	make one stitch see page 121
mm	millimeter(s)
oz	ounce(s)
p	purl
p2sso	pass two slipped stitches over, pass two slipped stitches over another stitch
p2tog	purl two stitches together, see page 121
patt	pattern
psso	pass slipped stitch over, pass a slipped stitch over another stitch

pwise	purlwise
rem	remain(ing)
rep	repeat
RH	right-hand
RS	right side
sl1(2)	slip one (two) stitch(es), from the left-hand needle to the right-hand needle without knitting it (them): see page 119
ssk	slip one stitch, slip one stitch, knit slipped stitches together, to decrease: see page 122
st(s)	stitch(es)
st st	stockinette (stocking) stitch
WS	wrong side
WT	with yarn at back, slip next stitch pwise from left-hand to right-hand needle. Bring yarn forward between needles. Slip stitch from the right-hand needle back to left-hand needle. Take yarn back between needles. Turn work.
yd	yard(s)
yo	yarnover, wrap yarn around needle between stitches, to increase and to make an eyelet: see page 120
[ ]	work instructions within square brackets as directed
*	work instructions after/between asterisk(s) as directed

suppliers

This is a list of some of the major suppliers of the yarns used in this book. For reasons of space, we cannot cover all stockists so please explore the local knitting shops and online stores in your own country. Please remember that from time to time companies will change the brands they supply or stock and will not always offer the full range. If you cannot find a particular yarn locally, there will usually be an excellent alternative and your local yarn store is the best place to ask about this, or visit www.yarnsub.com.

USA

Knitting Fever Inc.
www.knittingfever.com
Stockist locator on website
Debbie Bliss, Sirdar, Sublime

Jo-Ann Fabric and Craft Stores
Retail stores and online
www.joann.com
Stockist locator on website
Lion Brand

Lion Brand Yarns
Online store for Lion Brand yarns
Tel: +800 258 YARN (9276)
www.lionbrand.com
Stockist locator on website (USA, Mexico, and Canada)

WEBS
www.yarn.com
Sirdar, Sublime

Canada

Diamond Yarn
Tel: +1 416 736 6111
www.diamondyarn.com
Stockist locator on website
Debbie Bliss, Sirdar, Sublime

UK

Love Knitting
www.loveknitting.com
Online sales
Cascade, Red Heart, Rico, Rowan, Sirdar, Sublime

John Lewis
Retail stores and online
Tel: 03456 049049
www.johnlewis.com
Telephone numbers of stores on website
Debbie Bliss, Rowan, Sirdar, Sublime

Laughing Hens
Online store only
Tel: +44 (0) 1829 740903
www.laughinghens.com
Debbie Bliss, Rowan, Sublime

Australia

Black Sheep Wool 'n' Wares
Retail store and online
Tel. +61 (0)2 6779 1196
www.blacksheepwool.com.au
Debbie Bliss, Sirdar, Sublime

Sun Spun
Retail store only (Canterbury, Victoria)
Tel: +61 (0)3 9830 1609
Debbie Bliss, Rowan, Sublime

Finding a yarn stockist in your country
The following websites will help you find stockists for these yarn brands in your country. Please note that not all brands or types of yarn will be available in all countries.

Cascade Yarns
www.cascadeyarns.com
Stockist locator on website

DROPS Design
www.garnstudio.com

Red Heart
www.redheart.co.uk
www.redheart.com

Rico Design
www.rico-design.de

Rowan Yarns
Tel: +44 (0) 1484 681881
www.knitrowan.com

Sirdar (inc. Sublime)
Tel: +44 (0) 1924 231682
www.sirdar.co.uk

author acknowledgments

I would like to thank Cindy, Penny, Sally, Kerry, and everyone at CICO books for coming up with the idea for this book, and for being so supportive. I'd also like to thank my editor Kate Haxell, pattern checker Marilyn Wilson, photographer Terry Benson, and stylist Rob Merrett for being an incredible team. Thanks too to Louis, Louise, and Paddy, and especially to my husband, Roger, for his patience when things didn't go to plan. Finally, this book is dedicated to my father, David Goble (1925–2016), who wanted to be a writer himself and gave me the confidence to give it a go.

index